INTRODUCTION TO REFERENCE WORK IN THE DIGITAL AGE

JOSEPH JANES

NEAL-SCHUMAN PUBLISHERS, INC.

NEW YORK   LONDON

Published by Neal-Schuman Publishers, Inc.
100 Varick Street
New York, NY 10013

Printed and bound in the United States of America.

The paper used in this publication meets the minimum requirements of American National Standard for Information Sciences — Permanence of Paper for Printed Library Materials, ANSI Z39.48-1992. ♾

Library of Congress Cataloging-in-Publication Data

Janes Joseph, 1962–
    Introduction to reference work in the digital age / Joseph Janes
      p. cm.
    Includes bibliographical references and indexes.
    ISBN 1–55570–429–8 (alk. paper)
    1. Reference services (Libraries) 2. Internet in library reference services. 3. Electronic reference services (Libraries) I. Title.

Z711.J36 2003
025.5'24—dc21

2003052739

This book is dedicated with love to

Jeannette McFarland Janes,
her essence is on every page,

James and Leona Hartley,
both so dear to us all,

and

Jan Hartley,
my beloved, who has given me so much
and makes it all worthwhile.

Table of Contents

Preface

The world of reference work in libraries is changing, seemingly every day. In just the last few years, we've seen the rise of new resources, new storage media and formats for those resources, new technologies with which to use those media, and most important, new ways for the people we serve to be able to engage us. In many ways, the reference world of today looks like an entirely different planet from the one faced by our predecessors. Yet a careful reading of articles from the dawn of reference in the nineteenth century down to the last decade shows us that many of the problems, concerns, and issues we discuss aren't always all that new.

In *Introduction to Reference Work in the Digital Age*, I describe both the theory and the practice of reference today—the new technological domain as well as the new ideas, experiments, projects, and services that are being discussed and developed and theorized. I discuss what reference is *for* these days: what its niche is in librarianship and in the lives of our communities, how we can use things we've learned as a profession over the last century or so to our benefit, and how to think creatively and originally about more recent challenges and opportunities.

I also want to shake the profession's complacency level a bit. We're at a singular time here, perhaps even a unique one. I'm not sure the library world has ever faced so much change and dynamism from so many different quarters and in so many different directions in such profound and impactful ways. The stakes are high; I think we may well be at the crossroads between greater acceptance of, reliance on, and support for the work of librarians and libraries and the end of libraries as we know them. Too many people, especially those who hold our purse strings, ask, "Everything's on the Internet, so what do we need libraries for?" We've got to have a damned good answer for them. Now.

I wrote *Introduction to Reference Work* for multiple audiences. It's for students and other people who are new to the profession, unburdened by the notions of what has been but also inexperienced in the tools and tricks we of a certain age take for granted. I'm also writing to my colleagues in the reference world, people of my generation who've been around for a while and are wondering what to do now and how to do it in such a way that they recognize it as why they got into the reference business in the first place. I'm writing more broadly, too, to the entire professional community, adding my voice to those who want to move us all forward. My focus here is on how we can conceive of, design, develop, implement, and evaluate mediated information services for the people who live in our communities (geographic, academic, corporate, intellectual, and so on) so that those services are successful in satisfying their information needs. That covers a lot of territory, and it's important work that goes right to the heart of what libraries are for, present, past, and I hope, future.

I've spent a lot of time over the last several years thinking about reference and how it's changing. I started out in library school thinking I was going to be a reference librarian and somewhere along the way took a diversion into research and a doctoral program, eventually studying relevance—how people make decisions about documents and information. In the mid-1990s, I played a part in the genesis of the Internet Public Library, answering questions from all over the world, from people we never talked to and never saw. I got reengaged in library work and found myself drawn anew to the challenges and issues facing reference in the digital world.

Over the intervening years, I've been fascinated to watch this branch of my profession struggle with a new and emerging information environment, learn how to adopt it and adapt it to their work and vice versa, understand what it might mean, build things that would take advantage of it, and so on. Along the way, I've been struggling as well to figure out how to help people to learn how to be professionals in this area. The results of the work and thinking I've done, and the work and thinking of lots of other people, are now in your hands.

Introduction to Reference Work in the Digital Age opens with some thoughts about, and the history of, reference work, including why we do it, where we do it, and the values that underlie it. Chapter 2 examines the four essential concepts underpinning reference services: users, the communities in which they live, their information needs, and how we can best understand those needs, including the familiar and now sometimes not so familiar notion of the reference interview. Chapter 3 then discusses how we go about responding to those needs—by mediating and searching—and the ways in which responses are evolving. Chapter 4 takes on the technological realm, including current options, how to think about them, and some of the issues they raise. Chapter 5 explores the question of how reference practice is evolving to enfold the new environments and contexts and how we can prepare ourselves now and in the future to continue that evolution through training, staffing, and the like. Chapter 6 lays out a prototypical planning process for use in creating and, more important, *institutionalizing* an information service for any organization. In the final chapter, called "Syncope" (found in my trusty *Roget's International Thesaurus,* 5th edition, not the horrible dictionary version, but the one with the index to the thousand or so categories), I recapitulate the major themes and lay out a vision for how services might be reconceptualized.

Each of the chapters begins with an overview describing the scope of the material to be presented. At the end of each chapter, I've included "Questions for Review." These are questions that intrigue or stimulate or just plain bug me, and so I thought I'd share them and see if they intrigue or stimulate or bug you. I can imagine them being used not only as discussion questions in a classroom setting but also as starting points for debate or deliberation in a professional environment or even for personal reflection. It's not exactly *Chicken Soup for the Digital Reference Librarian's Soul* (I should sell as many books as they do), but I hope the questions spark interest regardless.

My goal with this book? I'd like you to come away with a better appreciation of the larger picture of where reference has been, where it is now, and where we as professionals can take it. Mainly, I want to help us all *think* about the field's challenges and issues, large and small, and how we can meet them professionally. Librarians have a long tradition of developing all sorts of tools and services to assist in our work: the library catalog, indexing and abstracting, the MARC protocol, reference work itself, literacy programs, the bibliography and other reference tools, thesauri, cooperative services such as OCLC—the list goes on. This is a proud heritage, and one we must continue.

I hope you find my ideas of help as we build upon and extend that powerful heritage into the exciting future of reference ahead.

Acknowledgments

THANKS

I'm something of a connoisseur of book acknowledgments. They're fascinating and often say as much about the author as the rest of the text. So make what you will of the following.

I've learned a lot about libraries and reference and how it all works from lots of people over the last 25 years or so, and I want to acknowledge my debts appropriately. It began in the Oneida Library in my hometown in central New York State. Betty Angelino (whose desk, bless her heart, groaned under the weight of nearly as many piles as does mine), Mildred Bramley, Norene Garlock, and Barb Thompson were all early role models of good reference practice. When I got to Syracuse University, I learned more from courses with the wonderful Antje Lemke and Leigh Estabrook, from both of whom I later shamelessly stole many of my best teaching tricks.

I've been teaching for over 15 years now, and I think I've learned nearly as much from my students at Syracuse and Michigan and Washington as they have from me; I thank them all for what they have given me. Most recently, my class on advanced information services at Washington was the source of a lot of great discussion that focused my thinking as I was writing; the framework for building and institutionalizing a service in Chapter 6 was taken directly from the assignment for the final projects my students so masterfully completed.

Once in a lifetime, if you're an educator and very, very lucky (it certainly wasn't from clean living), you have an experience in a class that transcends the three hours a week of instruction and the assignments. For me, that was the Internet Public Library project, which had its genesis in a graduate seminar at Michigan in 1995. It certainly changed my life and those of a few others as well. During that class and in the years I spent as director of the IPL afterward, I had the privilege of working with a group of people who amazed me every day with their hard work, enthusiasm, creativity, dedication, and humor. God, we had fun, and we did great stuff. In particular, I want to thank several people among the dozens who made that experience so powerful: David Carter, Nettie Lagace, Michael McClennen, Josie Parker, Sara Ryan, and Schelle Simcox from the original class, and who formed the core of what was to come, and then people such as Patricia Memmott, Bob Summers, Ken Irwin, Nicole Miller, Bryan Blank, and Deb DeGeorge. Lorri Mon occupies a special place in this list, and now in my life, as a doctoral student–colleague at Washington, from whom many more great things will be heard.

In the last few years, friends and colleagues in the Seattle area have done me the great honor of trusting my antiquated and rusty skills on their reference desks, and I believe I have kept my promise to them all that I wouldn't hurt anybody. My thanks go to Nancy Huling, Betsy Darrah, Anne Zald, and the other folks I have shared time with and learned from at the reference desk of Suzzallo Library at the University of Washington; ditto to Margaret Ellsworth and Bill Ptacek of the Bellevue Regional Library of the King County Library System, as well as to William Poore and the rest of the great staff of KCLS Answer Line service, from whom I learned how to do phone reference really fast if not half as well as they do. (And I got to wear the cool headsets!)

Gratitude also to my friends and occasional coconspirators among the digital reference community: Blythe Bennett, Steve Coffman, Paul Constantine, Donna Dinberg, Franceen Gaudet, Diane Kresh (who funded a lot of my initial research in this area and kick-started my research agenda), and all the folks at the Library of Congress; Buff Hirko and the Washington State VRS people; Dave Lankes and his crack staff at the Information Institute of Syracuse; Susan McGlamery, Nancy O'Neill, Donna Reed, Rivkah Sass, Matt Saxton, Pauline Lynch Shostack, Joanne Silverstein, Bernie Sloan, Sara Weissman . . . The list goes on and on. Their great work and ideas and examples have helped me to think better in lots of ways, and their friendship is greatly valued to boot. I've also gotten a lot out of my participation in the Virtual Reference Desk conferences, ALA and RUSA events, the DIG_REF listserv, and all the people I've met at conferences and meetings big and small where reference matters have been discussed.

I can't leave out people who actually helped in the writing and preparation of the manuscript and in my research work to date. Chrystie Hill, Alex Rolfe, Misha Stone, Melissa Weaver and Sarah Ellison all were of great help to me as my work progressed. Charles Harmon and Michael Kelley, my editors, have made the manuscript better from all their suggestions. Mike Eisenberg, my friend, colleague, and now dean—for encouraging me on this project and so much more.

Kris Bain, Scott Barker, Harry and Lorraine Bruce, Carol Eisenberg, Jodi Hartley, Karen Hiiemae, Ron Holmwood, Barbie and Doug Simchik, Margaret Taylor, Lisa and Terry Tubbs, the Woodcock family (Susie, Dave, Ashley, Abby, Matthew, Casey)—you know why.

And most important, thanks to two of the most extraordinary women I have ever known and, not coincidentally, the loves of my life. Words are inadequate to thank Jan Hartley, who has been in my corner in times good and bad and with whom I am privileged to share my life. No Jan, no book—it's just that simple.

I would not be who I am and what I am if it had not been for my mother, Jeannette McFarland Janes, a remarkable woman in so many ways. She always told me that I had good taste in the friends I chose, and in looking at the list above, I know once again—as always—that she was right.

Finally, in what can only be characterized as a goofy personal tradition, I offer the music that helped in writing the book: soundtrack albums from *Hedwig and the Angry Inch, Heavy*

Metal, Streets of Fire, Shrek, Moulin Rouge!, Flashdance, Velvet Goldmine, The Shadow, Strictly Ballroom, Restoration, and *The Princess Bride* and cast albums from *Chess, Candide,* and *Jesus Christ Superstar;* Fleetwood Mac, *Rumours* and *Greatest Hits;* Queen, *Classic Queen;* just about every Elton John album; Metallica, *Metallica;* the Wallflowers, *Bringing Down the Horse;* Live, *Throwing Copper;* Bonnie Tyler, *Faster Than the Speed of Night;* Abba, *Abba Gold; The Best of Culture Club;* healthy doses of Handel, Mozart, Elgar, and Brahms; Annie Lennox, *Diva;* Duran Duran, *Decade;* Yanni, *Live at the Acropolis;* Dire Straits, *Money for Nothing;* and of course, Meat Loaf, *Bat Out of Hell.*

Chapter 1

Reference, Digital and Otherwise

In this chapter, we'll discuss

- what *reference* has meant and been over the last century or so;
- the main features and aspects of reference work;
- what motivates those who do reference work;
- how societal and technological changes impact reference work;
- the role of values in reference; and
- how digital reference has revolutionized, and is revolutionizing, the ability of libraries to connect people with information.

WHAT IS REFERENCE?

Introduction to Reference Work in the Digital Age is about reference—it says so right in the title—and so it seems appropriate to start out by defining exactly what we mean when we say "reference." I can hear the groans now: "Oh, jeez, not another book from some pointy-headed academic who's got to define everything. What's next, the historical backdrop?" In fact, yes, the historical

1

backdrop follows presently, but I think it's important to ponder for just a minute what *reference* really is, because the next response is likely to be "C'mon, everybody knows what reference is." Let's see if that's true.

To look for definitions of *reference* (an intriguing reference inquiry in itself, no?), I thought immediately of two places: the Reference and User Services Association (RUSA), the division of the American Library Association (ALA) primarily dedicated to reference work and populated by reference librarians; and the major textbooks used in reference classes.

Reference According to RUSA

Apparently, reference is somehow tied to the notion of user services. The history of RUSA's very name is revealing. Prior to 1996, RUSA was known as the Reference and Adult Services Division, which itself was formed in 1972 in the merger of the Reference Services Division (RSD) and the Adult Services Division (ASD). In turn, the RSD came into being in 1957, when the reference sections of the divisions dedicated to public libraries and academic libraries combined with the ALA's Bibliography Committee. In the same year, the ASD emerged as "the Adult Education Section of the Public Library Division expanded to include . . . librarians in all types of libraries that serve adults.[1] Over the last half century, then, the notion of reference has grown to include education, encompassing various kinds of libraries—and, by extension, their users—and the needs of youths as well as adults. In the process, the ALA also finally came up with a group with a pronounceable acronym.

RUSA's Web pages contain nothing that explicitly defines *reference,* but a few sections help us to understand the association's view of the areas with which it deals. In the introduction to "Guidelines for Information Services," we find the following sentences:

> A library, because it possesses and organizes for use its community's concentration of information resources, must develop information services appropriate to its community and

in keeping with the American Library Association's Library Bill of Rights. These services should take into account the information-seeking behaviors, the information needs, and the service expectations of the members of that community. *Provision of information in the manner most useful to its clients is the ultimate test of all a library does.*[2] (emphasis added)

Clearly, this is a big deal if it's part of the ultimate test of the library's activity and operation, but it's a bit vague. Somewhat more specific language appears in the introductory paragraph of the Web page describing RUSA's organization:

The Reference and User Services Association is responsible for stimulating and supporting in every type of library the delivery of reference/information services to all groups, regardless of age, and of general library services and materials to adults. *This involves facilitating the development and conduct of direct service to library users, the development of programs and guidelines for service to meet the needs of these users, and assisting libraries in reaching potential users.*[3] (emphasis added)

This is somewhat better, broadly laying out what these services do and describing them as "direct," but again it's still somewhat nebulous. I went through the rest of the sections of RUSA's Web site that looked likely to give me a definition of *reference* and never found one, but there were lots of phrases that were variations on *direct services to users.*

Failing to find an answer for myself, I did what we all hope people will do: I asked. Cathleen Bourdon, the executive director of RUSA, very graciously (and quickly) answered my e-mail and told me that RUSA uses the American National Standard Z39.7 for its official definition of *reference:* "An information contact that involves the use, recommendation, interpretation, or instruction in the use of one or more information sources, or knowledge of such sources, by a member of the reference or information staff."

Reference According to Katz, Bopp, and Smith

I then turned to the two primary textbooks used in North American reference classes, William Katz's *Introduction to Reference Work,* now in its eighth edition, and Richard Bopp and Linda Smith's *Reference and Information Services: An Introduction,* now in its third. Katz, in his characteristically blunt style, opens his book thus: "Reference librarians answer questions" (2002: 1:3). That's certainly clear enough, but it does leave a bit to be desired. Later, he elaborates by describing the reference librarian as "the person who interprets the question, identifies the precise source for an answer, and, with the user, decides whether or not the response is adequate. The same librarian, when asked, will instruct the user on how to find information in an electronic or printed reference source" (2002: 1:10). In other discussions, he refers to reference librarians as "information mediator[s]" who "determine what is useful, what is needed, and what can be rejected" and says that where librarians are useful as mediators, they "will be absolutely necessary. . . . The reference librarian *selects what is relevant* and thereby helps tame the information giant" (2002: 2:26, emphasis in original).

Bopp and Smith open their book by saying, "In this text, the focus is both on personal assistance provided to individual library users (e.g., answering reference questions) and on organized services provided to groups of users (e.g., bibliographic instruction). Attention is also paid to behind-the-scenes activities, such as staff development and evaluation of reference services, which are necessary components of the provision of quality services" (2001: 3). They further state that the essence of reference services is "the provision of assistance to individuals seeking information and ideas" (6) and go on to enumerate a list of varieties of reference services:

- Information
  - Ready-Reference Questions
  - Bibliographic Verification
  - Interlibrary Loan and Document Delivery
  - Information and Referral Services
  - Fee-Based Services and Information Brokering[4]

- Guidance
  - Readers' Advisory Services
  - Bibliotherapy
  - Term-Paper Counseling
  - Selective Dissemination of Information
- Instruction
  - One-to-One Instruction
  - Group Instruction

Why Is It Called "Reference" Anyway?

A quick step back to basics: why is this called "reference" work in the first place? To be sure, a lot of *referring* goes on, to information, to people, to sources, and so on, but it's not immediately obvious why this should be called *reference* as opposed to, say, *information* work, or *question* work or *guidance* or anything else. I couldn't find any source, historical or contemporary, that gives an unequivocal answer to this. The term comes into common usage in the 1880s, but its genesis appears to be lost or at least well hidden.

By the 1940s, Hutchins was exploring the question of when *reference question* had become a term of art. Her inquiry focuses on the distinction between a *research* question and a *reference* question (still with me?), and she incorrectly gives 1899 as the date of the first article to use the term in the professional literature (1944: 16–17). A decade later, the historian of reference, Rothstein, rather tantalizingly offered this footnote about the early use of the word:

> The term "reference department" apparently meant no more at that time than the books which did not circulate. Cf. the *Eleventh Report* of the Chicago Public Library, 1883: "The reference department—by which term is now meant the books which do not circulate" (p. 20). It was not until the 1890's that the term came to be used consistently in its present sense. (1953: 5 n. 16)

The best I can surmise is that indeed the name of the service came from what we called the books we used. The *Oxford English Dictionary* gives the first usage of *book of reference* as 1836 and that of *reference library* as 1858. It would seem that the reference books were there first, and then it became more and more common for librarians to offer assistance in their use, the librarians' work gradually becoming known as *reference work*, and then their work extended to other aspects of direct service. Some ideas die hard, though; the ALA's *Glossary of Library Terms* as late as 1943 gives the first definition of *reference department* as "[t]he part of a library in which its reference books are kept for consultation" (Thompson, 1943: 113).

A BRIEF HISTORY OF REFERENCE

In the beginning, there was no reference. Or at least not like we understand it today. Several historians of reference have remarked that as reference is so commonplace, even expected, in the pantheon of library service today, it's difficult to imagine that it had to evolve, not to mention that it evolved relatively slowly.

The Nineteenth Century

Rothstein's excellent survey points out that the proceedings of the Librarians' Conference of 1853 make no mention of anything approaching reference service, shy of an oblique mention in one paper that librarians should have some idea what the library has and help people find things. The 1876 U.S. Department of Education report on the state of public libraries makes only "casual mention" of help to readers; indeed, it was felt that helping people was a distraction from more important work and therefore having a lot of reference books available was a good idea, so readers wouldn't bug the librarians (Rothstein, 1953: 3, 4)

Galvin, in his article on "Reference Services and Libraries" in the *Encyclopedia of Library and Information Science*, offers a broad perspective on the development of reference services. He points to larger forces, such as the increasing urbanization and industrialization of the United States; "the acculturation of a large immigrant population; the rise of public education; and the changing character of the American college and university" (1977: 211). The emerging public libraries were becoming increasingly concerned with the use of materials as opposed to just their collection and conservation, and university libraries were only beginning to be taken seriously as the nature of instruction changed and graduate study and research were becoming more common.

Galvin also notes the rapid and dramatic growth in the size of library collections in the last quarter of the nineteenth century. This increase helped to spur a time of great interest in the organization of those collections, specifically, the development of many new methods of cataloging and classification, such as those of Cutter and Dewey and Poole's 1882 index to periodical literature. Most librarians seemed to believe those systems were self-evident and thus were solving the problem of access: with the new systems, it shouldn't be hard at all for people to find what they were looking for.

Well, you've guessed the punch line by now—they couldn't. Fine as those systems were, they weren't enough. Hear the voice of someone who was there:

> I have not been unmindful . . . of the great value of the assistance rendered readers by certain catalogues, which have been issued lately. There is little danger of appreciating too highly such work as that for which we are indebted to Mr. Noyes, Mr. Cutter and Mr. Winsor. . . . I need not remind you, however, that many persons who use a library have to be instructed in regard to the use of catalogues, and need practice before they can use them to the best advantage. Entries are overlooked. Discrimination is lacking for separating good books from those of little merit. . . . *It frequently happens, also, that readers do not know under what general subject to look for a minute piece of information.* (Green, 1876: 78, emphasis added)

Wow. Every time I read this article, I'm struck by how contemporary it sounds. Get beyond the florid language, and the writer speaks to us today in terms we easily understand. Catalogs are fine, but the vast majority of people can't use them without help or training. The quote above is taken from the first article to appear in the library literature about reference, although the author doesn't use the term. The quote is from Samuel Swett Green, the director of the Worcester Free Public Library in Massachusetts, writing a version of a talk that he gave at a conference of librarians in 1876, which appeared in the first volume of *Library Journal*.

The first half of Green's article is filled with the sort of war stories reference librarians have delighted in for decades.

> A curious woman asked me a few months since to give her a book which would show what the "scollop" is. . . . It was only after an hour's search that I found out from Verrill and Smith's "Invertebrate Animals of Vineyard Sound and Adjacent Waters, etc.," that it is the 'central muscle which closes the valves' of a certain shell. (1876: 76–77)

Although it's easy to characterize his question-handling technique as patronizing, pun intended, there is also much we recognize as common reference practice today. He discusses

- helping people to search through tables of contents and indices (not unlike database or catalog searching today);
- evaluating information critically;
- helping people with consumer questions, such as how to buy the best lightning rod;
- not giving answers to medical or legal questions;
- selectively disseminating information, as by dropping a line to the chairman of a city government committee, telling him of a new book that would be of interest; and
- teaching people how to use dictionaries and encyclopedias and pointing out that they can often find answers for themselves.

He further suggests that librarians be pleasant and mingle freely with readers, that they not make readers dependent on them for help, and that they not give a point of view on political matters. This advice doesn't prevent librarians from guiding or giving advice or even telling people what they want; Green sees this as part of the library's mission to "brighten any glimmerings of desire that manifest themselves in lowly people to grow in culture or become better informed" (80), which in no small part is what motivated the public library movement in the first place.

Who will be good at this work? Green suggests people who are courteous, sympathetic, patient, cheerful, enthusiastic, persistent, and cordial and who have a democratic spirit. He also stresses the importance of what we would call readers' advisory, in one of my favorite passages from his article, which I indulge myself in quoting here at length:

> It is a common practice, as we all know, for users of a library to ask the librarian or his assistants to select stories for them. I would have great use made of this disposition. Place in the circulating department one of the most accomplished persons in the corps of your assistants—some cultivated woman, for instance, who heartily enjoys works of the imagination, but whose taste is educated. . . . It is well if there is a vein of philanthropy in her composition. Instruct this assistant to consult with every person who asks for help in selecting books. This should not be her whole work; for work of this kind is best done when it has the *appearance* of being performed incidentally. . . .
>
> The person placed in charge of this work must have tact, and be careful not to attempt too much. If an applicant would cease to consult her unless she gives him a sensational novel, I would have her give him such a book. Only let her aim at providing every person who applies for aid with the best book he is willing to read. (79, emphasis in original)

OK, enough of 1876; you get the picture. It's simultaneously reassuring and unsettling to know that we have so much in common with people of that day—it's nice to know that these issues aren't problems of our own making or environment but kind of

Figure 1.1 Reference Desk, Watertown Free Public Library, 1902. Reprinted with their kind permission.

scary that nobody seems to have solved them in 125-plus years of reference work. Read the whole Green article; it's been Web-ized at least once[5] so you can get it easily for free, and it's worth it.

The term *reference* is first seen in the literature in 1891, in an article in *Library Journal* (William Child's article on "Reference Work at the Columbia College Library"), and appears as an index term for the first time then as well. Child has a fairly broad definition of *reference*, saying that it involves "in short, doing anything and everything in [the librarian's] power to facilitate access to the resources of the library in his charge" (1891: 298). Galvin says that the first full-time reference position was established at Boston Public Library in 1883 (1977: 212), although he cites no source, but Rothstein's otherwise quite thorough history does not include this; the first such position he mentions are two reported by Dewey at Columbia College in an 1885 survey (Rothstein, 1953: 10).

Early reference work arose first in the public and special libraries, according to Bunge—the special libraries (largely governmental at first, then corporate) incorporating it as part of their mission to provide what he calls "amplified service" to their clientele and the public libraries doing so to make themselves useful and to help engender support (1983: 3). Development was slower in the college and university libraries, due "at least in part, to the expectation that faculty members and students should be able to find their own materials and information and to the emphasis the scholarly community placed on collection development and subject access to materials through cataloging" (3). It's interesting to note that the reference desk, that icon of service about which so much is said and has been debated, developed along with the increasing specialization and departmentalization of reference services between the two world wars; the desk is a relatively late aspect of reference work.

The Twentieth Century

Textbooks for instruction in reference began to appear quite early; the first of note is James Wyer's *Reference Work*, published in 1930 by the ALA, although the first edition of the association's *Guide to Reference Books* appeared in 1902. Wyer refers to the *Guide*, edited in those days by the estimable Isadore Gilbert Mudge, in explaining why he will not go into much detail on specific sources. His book is divided into three sections, on "Materials: The World of Print," "Methods: The Use of Print," and "Administration." The first section gives a broad overview of reference work, the types and study of reference books and materials, their acquisition and organization, and the role of interlibrary cooperation. In the second section, he discusses the search process in general and in two specific subject areas (chemistry and fine arts) and how reference work is conducted in the four major types of libraries (public, academic, school, special). The administration section discusses the qualifications of the reference librarian (the top five traits emerging from a survey of reference librarians were intelligence, accuracy, judgment, professional knowledge, and dependability; patience, forcefulness, and neatness came in lowest), the work of the reference department, and "training the public." It concludes with notes on rooms and furniture.

Wyer opens his second section, though, with perhaps the most interesting chapter, at least to a current audience, on handling reference questions. Here we get to the real meat, and there's nothing here to surprise an early twenty-first-century reference librarian. In particular, his sections describing the reference interview are a hoot. After an introductory section and a discussion of "the customer is always right," he describes the essential features of what we call the reference interview as mind reading and cross-examination. What reference librarian hasn't experienced this feeling? "You see they will choke to death and die with the secret in them rather than tell you what they want": Wyer quotes this from an article in the *Harvard Graduates Magazine* of 1922, as true today as it ever was (1930: 100). Wyer himself says, "Librarians have always marveled mightily at the invincible inarticulateness of inquirers." I love this bit:

> The reader who knows and can tell what he wants forms an encouraging proportion. He is a joy to serve or to show how to serve himself. The reader who does not know is almost incredibly numerous, generally honest and earnest, and worth working for and with. It is the reader who knows and won't tell, or who feels and doesn't know how to tell, who calls for mental treatment. (100–101)

Strong words, but he backs off a tad in the next section, on cross-examination. Here he goes through the familiar litany of what a librarian needs to know to respond to a question: what information is desired, in what format, and in what depth; how much is wanted; the level of treatment, from trivial to scholarly; when it is needed; and so on. There is precious little guidance, though, on how to get at all this: "[L]et it be neither brusque and abrupt not too businesslike. It should be marked by questions as few as possible but direct. Get the reader to talking and let him tell all you want if he will. Be receptively inquisitive but be sure the needed information is procured" (102). He also addresses the *why* question: "Strictly, this is not the library's business, but often it is volunteered, and no item of information is more helpful. If it does not come out otherwise, the question 'Do you mind saying what this is for, it will help very much in directing you to the best material?' will not often be resented" (102).

But in general, there is very little of the user here. A great deal of time is spent on sources and materials, their organization, searching, and use, the running of the service, and so on, and pretty short shrift is given to the actual people on the other side of the desk. This characterizes a great deal of reference instruction for a very long time, indeed; it forms a healthy chunk of the reference course I took in 1980, at least, and to tell the truth, I've taught classes with that focus as well.

The next major textbook of reference is that of Margaret Hutchins, also published by ALA, in 1944. Hutchins says quite clearly that her book is not a revision of Wyer's, and indeed, it is substantially different in structure and organization. She opens with a brief chapter on the meaning and context of reference work (following a quite charming and inspirational prefatory section describing how the wonders of reference librarianship change the life of a young college student and set him on the path to enlightenment, leading eventually to his choice of a faculty position at a university because of its strong library!). This is followed by a section on "Reference Questions," including chapters defining a reference question, discussing the reference interview and the technique and methods of answering questions, and providing specifics on answering several categories of questions (bibliographic, biographical, geographic, statistical). A section on the selection of materials of various types and formats follows, then sections on organization of reference materials, the organization and administration of the service, and the "less common functions of a reference librarian" (advising readers, teaching the use of books and libraries, reporting literature searches, working with interlibrary loan, and participating in public relations). She concludes with a chapter on evaluating reference work.

Of particular interest are her chapters on the interview and the technique of answering questions. Her discussion of the interview describes the success of a reference encounter as depending on the proper relationship among the questioner, the librarian, the sources, and the question itself: "If any of these relationships is slighted the work becomes lopsided. If the personal relationships are neglected, although a *correct* answer to the question may be found, it may nevertheless be unsatisfactory to the inquirer" (Hutchins, 1944: 21, emphasis in original). This is an intriguing model and could easily form the basis for thinking about the most appropriate way to evaluate reference service, leading us out of the accuracy-versus-satisfaction conundrum.

It is also illustrative of her tone and outlook. Hers is a much more user-centric view; she says that the reference librarian "needs to be *en rapport* with the person whom he is helping," that the "first requirement . . . is approachability, not only easy access physically, but easy intellectual and spiritual access as well," and that "[a]ssistance should not be forced on a reader. He may have a perfectly good reason for preferring to work out his problem by himself rather than take anyone into his confidence" (22). Contrast Wyer's descriptions of mind reading and cross-examination with this:

> So much has been said and written humorously . . . about the difficulties of getting readers to divulge their actual wants that there is danger of an assumption that [they] stupidly or willfully and perversely withhold information. Probably this is very seldom the case. More often the reader simply does not know how to state his needs clearly, or else is afraid of making a nuisance of himself. (Hutchins, 1944: 24)

A very different perspective indeed. Hutchins demonstrates throughout the book a real concern for people asking questions and the librarian's professional role in helping them. Her interviews must have been cordial and measured but almost sly in the way she got people to relax and share with her what they really wanted and why; she emphasizes rapport and cordiality as well as professionalism throughout. In fact, in her qualities for success as a reference librarian, she lists a good memory paired with a good imagination, mental flexibility, thoroughness, orderliness, persistence, and judgment (Hutchins, 1944: 32).

I think it would be overreaching to say that Hutchins's outlook represents some sort of tipping point over Wyer's, but it is true that later textbooks, such as those by Katz and Bopp and Smith, pay substantially more attention to the user than Wyer or certainly Green and his contemporaries did. This is not to say that later works don't spend a significant amount of time on sources and the "when to use *Current Biography* over *Who's Who*" sort of thing, but one does sense a subtle and gradual shift here. Memorization of the finer points of sources has been a part of reference instruction and training for a long time, and it won't die easily, but Hutchins opened an important door in helping budding reference librarians think about the object and motivation of their work.

The Present

One of the signal features of the history of reference work is the introduction and incorporation of new technologies in designing and delivering services. Ryan examines several such technological innovations—the use of mail, telephone, and Teletype in reference—and the discussion of each in the reference literature of its day. Some of this stuff is a scream. A 1936 discussion of telephone reference suggests librarians should not define "unsuitable" words, and a 1953 article includes this gem: "Abraham Lincoln walked twenty miles to borrow a book, but some of his fellow Americans of today want to reach for the telephone and have you read it aloud to them" (1996: 246). What would she have made of chat-based services pushing Web pages?

Ryan identifies several common features of these innovations. First of all, each of these technologies was in fact adopted and seen as an opportunity to provide better or fuller service to library patrons. But almost immediately, limitations, boundaries, policies, and restrictions were developed about how much service to provide, to whom, and under what circumstances (telephone services might be geared toward businessmen and not necessarily serve "clubwomen," for example), seemingly out of a fear of being overwhelmed or slighting people who had actually presented themselves at the desk for help. She also provides an intriguing example of a Teletype service also being used as a communication channel between librarians above and beyond its use as a reference-question shuttle, raising a parallel with the then-new use of the Internet (249).

Anybody reading this book who hasn't been in a coma or on Mars for the last few years certainly doesn't need to read me or other authors to know that things are changing in the information world these days. I think there was a time there when it was possible to pull the covers over your head and pretend maybe it would all go away, and I wouldn't be surprised if there are still more than a few among our colleagues who secretly hope that the world of 1985 (or earlier) will come back.

And to be honest, I understand where they're coming from. I graduated with my MLS in 1983, just when it began to be clear that technology was going to have a lot more to do with librarianship than anybody might have thought. Lots of libraries had computers in those days, though the microcomputer revolution was still just over the horizon. The larger libraries had automated their catalogs (remember the really early ones, with the little dot at the bottom center of the screen to simulate the hole in the catalog card?). OCLC was up and running with those miserable special-purpose terminals. We did online searches with curly thermal-paper printers over 300-baud dedicated dial-up lines. And microforms were still pretty keen. OK, you're right, microforms were never really keen. But you know what I mean.

That little burst of nostalgia reminds me at least that those of my fellow librarians who joined the profession much before I did weren't really prepared for a world of radical and constant change. I certainly wasn't. And let's face it, there have always been a significant number of people who went into this profession precisely because it *wasn't* going to change very much. To be sure, librarianship has to be somewhat conservative (with a small *c*) because one of our responsibilities is the preservation of the human record. So it isn't surprising that the profession can sometimes be a bit slow to adapt; there's a lot riding on what we do, and if we get something wrong—suppose we'd firmly bet on, say, microcards or the CD-ROM as an exclusive technology—we and the communities we serve could be in a deep hole, heritage-wise. This is not to say we haven't made a few missteps, but on the whole I think we've done rather well.

But now the stakes are significantly higher, change is coming more rapidly and from more sources, and the risks of doing nothing are greater. It may well be that the technological changes of the late twentieth and early twenty-first centuries will force libraries and librarians to completely overhaul a lot of what they do and how they do it or face an increasingly irrelevant future. It might be somewhat less dramatic than that. But I think it's pretty difficult to argue at this stage that these changes won't be of major and enduring significance for a profession that has always been involved with the technologies involved in storing, organizing, retrieving, and using information.

The Future

I'll spare you the laundry list of "The Profound Changes That Will Affect Us All," but here are a few goodies for your consideration:

- The 2000 Census shows that a 53 percent increase in the number of people of Mexican origin fueled much of the increase of nearly 13 million in the Hispanic population between 1990 and 2000[6] and that the median age of the U.S. population was 35.3 years, the highest it has ever been. The increase in the median age reflects the aging of the baby boomers. However, the 65-and-over population actually increased at a slower rate than the overall population for the first time in the history of the census.[7]
- Nearly one in five persons—53 million—said they had some level of disability in 1997, while one in eight—33 million—reported they had a severe disability, also according to the Census Bureau.[8]
- Between 1995 and 1999, the percentage of public schools with Internet access increased from 50 percent to 95 percent.

In 1999, two out of three public school teachers used computers or the Internet for classroom instruction.[9]

- In 1998, at least 66 percent of all holders of a graduate or first professional degree used the Internet. Next were holders of a bachelor's degree: 59 percent of this group used the Internet. Among holders of an associate degree, 43 percent used the Internet, as did 42 percent of persons with some college. Among persons with a high school diploma or the equivalent, 21 percent used the Internet, while just 7 percent of those without a high school diploma used it. In part, individuals with higher levels of educational attainment are most likely to use the Internet because they were often exposed to computers and the Internet as students and are therefore better equipped with the necessary skills to go online. Also, holders of advanced degrees may have more opportunities to access the Internet. Many jobs that require advanced degrees also have higher rates of Internet use.[10]

- Despite the slowdown that has hit the U.S. economy, more laborers and factory workers than members of any other segment of the population went online for the first time in the last year, according to a report released by Nielsen// NetRatings. The report found that 9.6 million blue-collar workers were online as of March 2001, up from 6.2 million in March 2000. That rate of growth—52 percent—is more than twice the rate of overall Internet-usage growth, according to Nielsen//NetRatings' measurements. These users spent an average of 11 hours online and viewed 698 Web pages in March 2001, spread across an average of 18 sessions on the Internet. The second fastest growing group of Net users was homemakers, who saw a 49 percent jump, to a total online population of 2.5 million. Service workers were online to the tune of 2.9 million, 37 percent higher than the year before. Salespeople also saw their ranks swell, by 37 percent, to 5.6 million users. Professionals form the largest single category of Internet users, according to NetRatings' measurements, at 18.5 million, up 23 percent. There were 14.4 million executives or managers using the Internet, for a 21 percent rise, and 8.5 million retirees, up 28 percent.[11]

- According to a 2000 study of public libraries and the Internet, nearly all public library outlets, 95.7 percent, have Internet connections, an increase in connectivity from 83 percent in 1998;
  - suburban connectivity increased from 88.1 percent in 1998 to 98.5 percent in 2000;
  - rural connectivity increased from 78.4 percent in 1998 to 93.3 percent in 2000;
  - 60.4 percent of outlets offer access to online database-subscription services at all workstations; and
  - 36.1 percent offer remote access to online database services.[12] .

So we already knew that technology was getting faster, bigger, and cheaper seemingly by the minute, but it isn't all about technology. There are significant demographic, educational, and economic shifts going on as well, which will necessarily affect libraries and the way they do their business. In addition to these trends, consider these shifts:

- the move to the Web of traditional information sources (britannica.com, for instance, although that's not a story anybody's proud of so far) and its use as an enabling mechanism for delivering catalogs, databases, and a variety of other services from established sources such as Gale, ProQuest (neé UMI), LexisNexis, and so on, though sad old Dialog appears not to have been able to get out of its own way enough to be much of a player here,
- the rise of native Web resources, such as the Internet Movie Database, Yahoo!, amazon.com, Web logs, zines, and so on,
- an aging and graying profession with significant concerns about replacing itself with a new generation of librarians[13] who bring quite different backgrounds, experiences, outlooks, and training to their work—

and you get the recipe for a pretty interesting world, indeed.

WHY LIBRARIES OFFER REFERENCE SERVICES

The motivations behind reference work have already come up in a few places in the preceding discussion, but I thought it was worth a separate discussion to make clear why reference was such a good idea in the first place and why it still is.

Bopp and Smith see reference as originating "partially in response to one of that era's most important accomplishments: the spread of education" (2001:5). More people were educated, educational institutions grew, and the size and complexity of academic libraries grew with them; combine this with new requirements to use the library in that education, and spill those educated people over into their public libraries, and you get a greater need for an intermediary skilled in helping people find information.

Katz, as we might expect, puts things in somewhat more succinct terms: "What is the single biggest problem concerning information today? There is too much of it" (2002: 2:16). This begins his discussion of the reference librarian as information mediator. And librarians are also navigators "of an information highway which increasingly becomes more labyrinthine. Tortuous to follow, to discover the on- and off-ramps, the information highway's perplexities require an experienced, intelligent guide. The reference librarian is that guide" (2002: 1:3).

So not only is there a lot of information, but it's really hard to find.

Green in effect makes the same claims in 1876. Galvin points to two other historical motivations, in addition to providing assistance and instruction to students and becoming an active force in education, both of which come directly from Green as well. He also echoes Green's views on what we now know as readers' advisory and what Galvin characterizes as elevating the popular reading taste, derived from the notion of the public library as the "people's university" (1977: 212–13).

Finally, and perhaps most immediately of interest today, is the notion that doing reference—helping people—makes the people who receive the help feel better about the library and therefore more likely to support it. Green writes that "the conviction spreads through the community that the library is an institution of such beneficent influences that it cannot be dispensed with" (1876: 78). From his pen to the ears of the gods.

The RUSA Web site gives us the following in the introductory section of the "Guidelines for Information Services":

> Libraries have an inherent obligation to provide information service to support the educational, recreational, personal and economic endeavors of the members of their respective communities, as appropriate to the libraries' individual missions. Information services in libraries take a variety of forms including direct personal assistance, directories, signs, exchange of information culled from a reference source, reader's advisory service, dissemination of information in anticipation of user needs or interests, and access to electronic information.[14]

This is interesting indeed, because now no longer is reference a nice idea or a shrewd political move or a helpful appendix to a well-stocked library. It's *inherent* in being part of a library and includes lots more than reactively answering questions.

I want to add an idea of my own here, and while it's certainly not original, it doesn't come up much in the reference literature. I found a mention in Wyer, in a section curiously headed "Mechanism versus Humanism": "Reference work exists because it is not possible to organize books so mechanically, so perfectly, as to dispense with personal service in their use" (1930: 5).

We know that among the sources of information most people consult initially when faced with a problem are their own things: their own files, hard disks, piles of paper, notebooks, directories, and so on. Why? Yes, because they're familiar and their own, but also because they organized them *for themselves* and thus it's comparatively easy for them to find things there. Anyone who knows me knows that I operate on what might charitably be called a geologic filing system: piles everywhere, occupying every flat surface, seemingly a jumble of just stuff. You should see what's surrounding me as I write this. (I completely don't get people with clean offices. How do they get anything done?)

Anyway, it's not a jumble to me. I know exactly where everything is and can find almost anything within about 60 seconds, based on which pile it's in, how long it's been there and, therefore, how far down it is, and, probably, the color or the kind of paper it's on, whether it's handwritten or printed, and so on. Drives some people nuts, but it works for me, and I think most people have their own similarly idiosyncratic systems.

But that's precisely why they work—because they're idiosyncratic. As organizational systems have to contend with larger numbers of people (families, departments, organizations, governments, and so on), they get more chaotic because they get further from what any individual would have made up for himself or herself and thus are increasingly foreign and difficult to use. People are no longer adapting the information to the way they work; it's the other way around. Build a way for everybody to have her or his own way of organizing information, and you can rule the world.

So let's imagine the worst possible case: a large store of information and a set of organizational systems that are designed to appeal to the broadest set of people possible—namely, everybody. We have a convenient name for such a storage place: the library. Sure, *we* understand LCSH and DDC and MARC and thesauri and indices and the like, but we built the stupid things. For everybody else in the world, they're the artifacts of the most difficult way to get at information imaginable, and it's a wonder anybody ever finds anything without an MLS. And it's also no wonder they find the Internet so appealing, because all they have to do is type what they want in the little box, and out comes the answer. We know that the answers they get are wrong or suboptimal, but most people don't know that, most of them don't care, and most of all, it was *easy*. Now that we've ladled the Internet on top of the preexisting library information systems, it only gets more confusing while seemingly it's gotten much easier, at least from the user's perspective.

In this Dantesque scenario, the need for professional, principled assistance looms ever more vital. Provided we can get it right.

THE VALUES BEHIND REFERENCE WORK

I use the word *principled* when discussing what kind of help is needed in this ever-emerging information world. That is not a casual usage; I want to address the question of the values underlying reference work. There's been a lot of discussion in professional periodicals and conferences and such about the need for a return to, or reinvigoration of, the traditional values of librarianship, along with core competencies and the like. For example, among the actions of the Congress on Professional Education (COPE) in 1999 was the formation of a task force on core values, which I'm sure made everybody feel better but seems to have had little if any effect on anything anybody is doing.

Yet of course values are important, and they should absolutely form part of the underpinning of a professional enterprise such as reference. I want to spend a little while, then, examining what's been said about values to see if we come to any conclusions.

Let's start with the general and look first at that task force's results, as found on the ALA Web site (this is marked as the fifth draft, April 2000):

> The library and information profession is enriched by the skills and knowledge of its individual members. Through their specialized training and experience, they contribute to the varied missions of their institutions and organizations. Over time, they have refined their services to meet the unique and ever changing needs of their communities. Despite the multiplicity of these skills and roles, librarians and information specialists hold the following values in common:
>
> - Connection of people to ideas
> - Assurance of free and open access to recorded knowledge, information, and creative works
> - Commitment to literacy and learning
> - Respect for the individuality and the diversity of all people
> - Freedom for all people to form, to hold, and to express their own beliefs
> - Preservation of the human record

- Excellence in professional service to our communities
- Formation of partnerships to advance these values[15]

Well, there's nothing objectionable here, but I suppose that's the nature of these things. The task force itself acknowledged that these were quite general, but it was trying to come up with a concise and simple set of values for the whole of the profession, not just for reference. It's a good start.

Next, let's look at another recent and signification contribution to the discussion of the values of the profession, from Michael Gorman's award-winning book on the matter. He distills a number of other writings and discussions into a set of eight central, or core, values of librarianship. (I've edited his second-level bullets a bit for space; the ones I left I thought were particularly of interest or necessary to clarify his values, and I hope I haven't altered his meaning or misrepresented his thoughts.)

- Stewardship
  - Preserving the human record to ensure that future generations know what we know
  - Caring for and nurturing of education for librarianship so that we pass on our best professional values and practices
  - Being good stewards of our libraries so that we earn the respect of our communities
- Service
  - Ensuring that all our policies and procedures are animated by the ethic of service to individuals, communities, society, and posterity
- Intellectual freedom
- Rationalism
  - Organizing and managing library services in a rational manner
  - Applying rationalism and the scientific method to all library procedures and programs
- Literacy and learning
- Equity of access to recorded knowledge and information

- Privacy
- Democracy
  - Playing our part in maintaining the values of a democratic society
  - Participating in the educational process to ensure the educated citizenry that is vital to democracy
  - Employing democracy in library management (2000: 26–27)

An engaging list, as we would expect from Michael Gorman, and one that overlaps, as we would expect, the COPE list. (While he was a member of the task force, he did not participate in the development of the draft but did comment on its development and revisions.) I'm particularly intrigued by "rationalism" and pleased with his placement of education for librarianship under "stewardship," where I concur it rightly belongs.

RUSA has an extensive list of values, presumably for the association as a whole, on its Web site, in the introductory section of the page on policies and procedures, intended for people new to offices of the association:

- We believe in universal access to information in a wide variety of formats.
- We value collections and information sources of the highest possible quality.
- We believe in reading as fundamental to quality of life and value all activities that promote it.
- We value the provision of innovative services and programs that meet the changing information needs of diverse populations.
- We value continuous evaluation and improvement in the management and delivery of collections and services to users.
- We value the professional growth and development of reference and user services staff.
- We value the role of reference and user services staff as educators in creating lifelong learners and critical thinkers.
- We value the unique contributions that human beings bring to the process of connecting users with the information they need.[16]

I have to admit I find this last one rather curious, feeling the need to defend the role of us mere humans in all of this, but given everything that's happened and been talked about in the last couple of decades (go read some of the digital library stuff about "automated reference librarians"—hoo, boy), I can understand where this came from.

Katz never really addresses the issue of values per se but does discuss two items in his section on ethics that seem relevant here: the confidentiality and privacy of library records and freedom of information (2002: 2:187–88). It is interesting to note that in the seventh edition of his book, these two are joined by reference accuracy (1997: 2:241–42), but it no longer appears in the eighth edition.

Finally, we take a look at the work of Ferguson and Bunge. In their article, they propose a series of "service values for the largely digital library," saying that libraries "would do well periodically to rethink their core values and to bring into awareness new values that match users' evolving needs and expectations" (1997: 258). The values they discuss are

- integration of technologies into librarianship, exploring "more adaptive service delivery configurations that will meet [user] needs in the present and yet possess inherent flexibility for the inevitable shift away from paper;"
- holistic computing, including connectivity but also electronic bibliographic tools, network-navigation and communication tools, and productivity tools to build, manipulate, and deliver research products;
- the delivery of core reference and instructional services through the network at the time of need, whenever that may be;
- making technology work for everyone, allowing ubiquitous access to value-added services, including consulting, tiered services, and active engagement with users and communities; and
- collaboration across administrative lines, here referring largely to computing and library functions in an academic environ-

ment but by inference similarly referring to any organizational context.

Ferguson and Bunge further stress the importance of constants, or "enduring basics," to be used as guideposts in building such services: users, their needs, and design based on knowing these; the scholarly communication system; the "continuing need of information users for assistance in gaining access to information sources"; equity and equal access to information; freedom of choice for users; and intellectual and academic freedom. (1997: 263)

Well, there's a lot here, and it's tempting to try to wrap these up in a neat bundle of three or five core core values, but I think that misses the point. The fact that there is significant overlap here (many mentions of intellectual freedom, equality of access, and privacy, for example) as well as unique things (stewardship, accuracy, collaboration) tells me that there's a rich fount of values at work in this domain, and it would be foolhardy—not to mention nigh impossible—to artificially compress them.

The point I'd like to leave this section with is this: in the kind of dynamically and radically changing environment we find ourselves in now, if we don't have values to anchor us, we're in deep trouble and might as well give up. There are some values that are seemingly universal, others that might be of more or less interest or salience in particular contexts or worlds. I don't want to say that it doesn't matter which ones any individual or organization picks; I want to say that it matters a whole hell of a lot, but they should be chosen thoughtfully, deliberately, and professionally and first, before much else is done in design, development, revision, or evaluation of a reference service.

DIGITAL REFERENCE

OK, so what is this digital reference thing, anyway? You've likely read or seen things about it, heard it talked about in conferences, perhaps even done it yourself in one way or another. But what is it? Where does it fit in? What should we be doing? What *shouldn't* we be doing? Are we behind? Will this all blow over? What software should we buy? So many questions. Here are some descriptions of digital reference:

- Digital reference is a librarian in a small town offering to follow up a reference question at her desk with an e-mail message because she can't quite satisfy every part of it right there on the spot.
- It's an academic library taking inquiries from its academic community via a Web form and responding by e-mail or calling or faxing or sending materials or setting up an appointment for a research consultation or all of these in whichever combination seems to make the most sense.
- It's a collaborative arrangement of several libraries working together and using call-center software to provide live, synchronous, chat-based service to their patrons.
- It's even QuestionPoint (QP), spearheaded by Diane Kresh and others at the Library of Congress and now supported also by OCLC, trying to build an international framework to support the highest caliber of information services.
- It's also Ask Joan of Art!, a service of the Smithsonian American Art Museum (and, parenthetically, one of the great names in the ask-an-expert biz, thanks in no small part to Joan Stahl, who felicitously founded it), answering e-mail questions about American art.
- It's people in a variety of commercial ask-an-expert services, such as Google Answers and About and AskMe and Abuzz and dozens and hundreds of others answering questions for fee or free because they want to and can.
- It's the Virtual Reference Desk project at Syracuse University, trying to bring some order and quality to the chaos that is the ask-an-expert world.

Digital reference is a pretty dynamic and exciting place, but there are also some things here to make your blood run cold. I know of at least one case where a scientific question posed to an ask-an-expert service run out of a major university got a response couched in the responder's thoroughly Christian beliefs, no doubt deeply held but wildly inappropriate.

Defining Digital Reference

So how about a definition of *digital reference*? Well here's one: *the use of digital technologies and resources to provide direct, professional assistance to people who are seeking information, wherever and whenever they need it.* I made this up, and it's not perfect, but it appears to capture the important concepts underlying the work and thinking about digital reference to date.

But let's stop and take a closer look at this definition. The middle part, about providing direct, professional assistance to people seeking information, seems pretty familiar, and in fact I adopted many of those words from the definitions of *reference* we began with. I should be clear that I also interpret *assistance* as including both the education of people about searching for and using information intelligently and the use of guidance-type services, such as readers' advisory.

The beginning refers to the use of digital technologies and resources, which is all fine and wonderful, but as we've already seen, reference librarians have been pretty good about adopting and adapting new technologies and new resources all along, so while that part of the definition calls attention to these technological advances, perhaps it's not strictly necessary.

The end, though, "wherever and whenever they need it," is new and deserves a bit more thought. This is virgin territory, at least to the library reference world. Other information services, like telephone directory services, information hotlines, and the like, have always been round-the-clock services, but few libraries have gone this route. To do this represents a real stepping up in level and quantity of service, not to mention a potentially large investment in staff and other resources. It also seems to me to be just not quite right; there may well be digital reference services that aren't synchronous, as many currently are, and it misses an important point about location. Part of the allure of digital reference services, both for people with questions and for librarians, is the ability to get (or provide people with) help not only wherever they are but also at the moment when they recognize they need some help.

So let's revise our definition, dropping the opening clause as unhelpful and rewording the ending. This leaves us with *the provision of direct, professional assistance to people who are seeking information, at the time and point of need.*

Not bad at all. But look at it. Now the technology is gone, but it has left a trace in "the time and point of need." Our definition is now independent of any specific technology, though wholly dependent on technology by implication (as reference always has been, or should have been), and yet commits services at the users' convenience and on their terms. Which seems to me to be what we've been trying to do ever since Green's day. Reference.

That's why this is not a book about digital reference; it's a book about reference, and all that entails about service, values, users, and all the rest.

THAT WHICH WE CALL "REFERENCE" IS AT A CRUCIAL TURNING POINT

This is the end of the beginning of the book and, I would say, also of reference itself. What we've been doing for the last century and a quarter seems to me to be preparation for what is to come. And that's the opportunity to start over, to generate and play with new ideas and revisit old ones, design services and models and ways of thinking about serving people at the time and point of *their* needs, and to do all of this based on and taking advantage of everything we've learned over the decades about what works and what doesn't in the reference endeavor. We have the chance to reinterpret the functions, motivations, and values of reference work in the light of this constantly changing and emerging information environment.

This is tremendously exciting work and also scary and pretty risky stuff.

I'd like to convey to my colleagues in the reference profession a few things in this book. First of all, it's really not that scary, and in many ways this is—and has to be—an adaptation of familiar practices and processes to a new environment. Second, we've made this kind of transition before, incorporating, for example, the telephone into reference, once a different and off-putting medium for communication, and in fact these technologies opened up new ways of serving people we already had been serving, not to mention lots of people we weren't and haven't been serving, and perhaps even couldn't serve. Also, these technologies are not a panacea and need to be approached thoughtfully and *professionally* to find out what works for us, what makes sense where and for whom and why. And finally, to be blunt, the clock is ticking, and if we don't get off our butts and do something meaningful and quickly, we'll be bypassed and ignored and left at the reference desk waiting for people who aren't coming, listening to the silence everybody else thinks we prize so highly but in fact is our death knell.

A while ago, I was on a panel at a session at an ALA conference, and the moderator asked me if I had a wake-up call for reference. As you may have already guessed, I have several, and I found the first one that popped into my head was "Google works." I'd never really thought of that before, but it rang true then and still does today. I happen to really like Google and have for some time; I usually get quite good results, and it seems to get slightly better rather than worse with time, as have so many other search engines or finding tools on the Net. Some day, I'm sure, it will start to creak or be replaced or supplanted by something better, but let's use it at the moment as the representative of quick and easy access to tolerably good stuff on the Internet.

Google is what we've been wanting for decades: a quick, free way to put in a few words and often get back something that is at least somewhat related to what we were looking for and that sometimes is exactly what we wanted. I can imagine people have difficulty framing their needs and using the best words, and can get thousands of irrelevant results in a Google search, but it does work pretty darn well.

Which seems to leave a profession dedicated to helping people find stuff in a bit of a pickle. If it works, what do we do? The concern about dropping reference statistics is rooted in no small part in this question. I think three courses of action are open to us in a Google-fied world:

1. Wait them out. If we believe that the Internet, Google, Yahoo!—all of it—is a passing fad, then all we have to do is wait long enough for people to realize that the good stuff, the quality information, is waiting for them in their friendly local library, and they'll eventually make their way back. Riiiiiiight.
2. Use Google. Well, that's what we're doing now when it seems to make sense; Google is certainly one of my favorite reference tools now, along with *The World Almanac* and *The American Heritage Dictionary* and *Britannica*. But there's got to be something more to it . . .
3. Figure out what we can do that Google can't or won't, do that as well as it can be done, publicize the bejesus out of it, and reinvigorate the professional role of reference librarians in the popular mind and our own self-image.

I vote for item 3, with item 2 thrown in as part of the arsenal. In the chapters to come, we'll see what sense we can make of all this and figure out what we can best do next.

QUESTIONS FOR REVIEW

- Will the use of an expanded set of technologies expand the "variety of services" discussed on pages 4–5?
- There's been discussion about the future role, if any, of the reference desk in the reference function for several years now. What conditions would make a library feel it's necessary or desirable to do away with it altogether?
- It seems that over time, discussions of reference service have focused increasingly on the user (as opposed to the librarian, sources, and so on). At what level is this a reflection of a rapidly changing service environment, which is difficult to keep a handle on?

- Each of us has our own constellation and ranking of values we think are most important in the way we conduct reference work. What's yours?
- We did adopt the telephone as a means of answering questions, but it was discussed in the professional literature on and off for over two decades. Is the ground more fertile now for technological innovation? Why?

ENDNOTES

1. Largely from Reference and User Services Association, "RUSA Guide to Policies and Procedures"/"Introduction"/"History." Available at: www.ala.org/rusa/guideintro.html.
2. Reference and User Services Association, "Guidelines for Information Services"/"Introduction." Available at: www.ala.org/rusa/stnd_consumer.html.
3. Reference and User Services Association, "RUSA Organization." Available at: www.ala.org/rusa/org.html.
4. In the second edition, "Research Questions" and "Database Searches" were also in this category (Bopp and Smith, 1995: 9–10).
5. At http://dlis.gseis.ucla.edu/people/jrichardson/personal.htm, for example.
6. U.S. Census Bureau, "Census 2000 Paints Statistical Portrait of the Nation's Hispanic Population," *U.S. Department of Commerce News,* May 10, 2001. Available at: www.census.gov/Press-Release/www/2001/cb01–81.html.
7. U.S. Census Bureau, "Nation's Median Age Highest Ever, but 65-and-Over Population's Growth Lags, Census 2000 Show," *U.S. Department of Commerce News,* October 10, 2001. Available at: www.census.gov/Press-Release/www/2001/cb01cn67.html.
8. U.S. Census Bureau, "Nearly 1 in 5 Americans Has Some Level of Disability, U.S. Census Bureau Reports," *U.S. Department of Commerce News,* April 3, 2001. Available at: www.census.gov/Press-Release/www/2001/cb01–46.html.
9. U.S. Census Bureau, *2001 Statistical Abstract of the United States,* 156. Available at: www.census.gov/prod/2002pubs/01statab/stat-ab01.html.
10. U.S. Department of Labor, "Internet Use Highest for Most Educated," *Monthly Labor Review: The Editor's Desk,* January 9, 2001. Available at: http://stats.bls.gov/opub/ted/2001/Jan/wk2/art02.htm.
11. Sam Costello, "Internet Use Rises among Blue-Collar Workers," IDG News Service, April 12, 2001. Available at: www.nwfusion.com/news/2001/0412bluecollar.html.

12. John Carlo Bertot and Charles R. McClure, "Public Libraries and the Internet 2000: Summary Findings and Data Tables." Paper submitted to the National Commission on Libraries and Information Science, Washington, D.C., September 7, 2000. NCLIS Web-release version available at: www.nclis.gov/statsurv/2000plo.pdf.
13. See, for example, Mary Jo Lynch, "Reading 65: Lots of Librarians Will Be There Soon," *American Libraries* (March 2002): 55–56.
14. Reference and User Services Association, "Guidelines for Information Services"/"Introduction." Available at: www.ala.org/rusa/stnd_consumer.html.
15. American Library Association, "Librarianship and Information Service: A Statement on Core Values," 5th draft, April 28, 2000. Available at: www.ala.org/congress/corevalues/draft5.html.
16. Reference and User Services Association, "RUSA Guide to Policies and Procedures"/"Introduction"/"Values." Available at: www.ala.org/rusa/guide_intro.html.

REFERENCES

Bopp, Richard E., and Linda C. Smith. 1995. *Reference and Information Services: An Introduction.* 2nd ed. Englewood, Colo.: Libraries Unlimited.

Bopp, Richard E., and Linda C. Smith. 2001. *Reference and Information Services: An Introduction.* 3rd ed. Englewood, Colo.: Libraries Unlimited.

Bunge, Charles A. 1983. "The Personal Touch: A Brief Overview of the Development of Reference Services in American Libraries." In *Reference Services: A Perspective,* edited by Sul Lee. Ann Arbor, Mich.: Pierian Press.

Child, William B. 1891. "Reference Work at the Columbia College Library." *Library Journal* 16.

Ferguson, Chris D., and Charles A. Bunge. 1997. "The Shape of Services to Come: Values-Based Reference Service for the Largely Digital Library." *College & Research Libraries* 58, no. 3 (May): 252–65.

Galvin, Thomas J. 1977. "Reference Services and Libraries." *In Encyclopedia of Library and Information Science.* Vol. 25. New York: Marcel Dekker.

Gorman, Michael. 2000. *Our Enduring Values: Librarianship in the 21st Century*. Chicago: American Library Association.

Green, Samuel S. 1876. "Personal Relations between Librarians and Readers." *Library Journal* 1 2/3: 74–81.

Hutchins, Margaret. 1944. *Introduction to Reference Work*. Chicago: American Library Association.

Janes, Joseph, and Chrystie Hill. 2002. "Finger on the Pulse: Librarians Describe Evolving Reference Practice in an Increasingly Digital World." *Reference & User Services Quarterly* 42, No. 1 (autumn): 54–65.

Katz, William A. 1997. *Introduction to Reference Work*. 7th ed. 2 vols. New York: McGraw-Hill.

Katz, William A. 2002. *Introduction to Reference Work*. 8th ed. 2 vols. New York: McGraw-Hill.

Rothstein, Samuel. 1953. "The Development of the Concept of Reference Service in American Libraries, 1850–1900." *Library Quarterly* 23, no. 1: 1–15.

Ryan, Sara. 1996. "Reference Service for the Internet Community: A Case Study of the Internet Public Library Reference Division." *Library and Information Science Research* 18, no. 3 (summer): 241–59.

Thompson, Elizabeth H. 1943. *A.L.A Glossary of Library Terms*. Chicago: American Library Association.

Wyer, James I. 1930. *Reference Work: A Textbook for Students of Library Work and Librarians*. Chicago: American Library Association.

Chapter 2

Understanding Users, Communities, and Their Needs

In this chapter, we'll discuss

- current ways in which people seek information, with and without assistance;
- the importance of recognizing—and planning for—the communities to which users belong and their unique information needs; and
- the traditional and digital techniques reference librarians use to help people state and refine their information needs.

A few vignettes illustrating how people get their information and resources today:

- A major telephone survey of several thousand Americans, conducted in the spring of 2000, found, among other things, that 40 percent of the survey population used both their public libraries and the Internet; that both library users and Internet users were younger, were better educated, and had higher incomes than nonusers of each; and that users of both were discriminating in their decisions on which to use for what. Specifically, the library received higher ratings on ease of use, low cost, availability of paper copy, accuracy and helpfulness of the librarians. The Internet received higher ratings on ease of getting there, time to get there, hours of access, range of resources, expectation of finding what is sought, ability to act immediately on the information obtained, currency of the information, fun, enjoyability of browsing, and the ability to work alone.[1]

- Paul Constantine, until recently head of Reference Services at the Olin-Kroch-Uris Libraries at Cornell University (and now at the University of Washington), described his undergraduate student population this way at a meeting once: "They do their banking via ATMs. They listen to music off CDs, but also from MP3 files they've downloaded from Napster or ripped from a CD, and burn their own CDs to boot. They communicate with their faculty often by e-mail and with their friends by instant messaging and chat software. They talk on cell phones."

- According to their June 2001 Form 10–K filing with the Securities and Exchange Commission (SEC), Ask Jeeves got 3.7 million questions a day from 11.9 million unique visitors to its site in December 2000, up from 2.6 million questions a day from 5.3 million visitors in December 1999.[2] Search Engine Watch reports that 100 million searches a day were performed on Google as of April 2001.[3] And in their SEC 10–K filing for 2000, Yahoo! reported that in December of 2000, their 180 million unique users "viewed an average of approximately 900 million Web pages per day on Yahoo!-branded online properties."[4]

- A study conducted on behalf of Keen.com tracked 74 adults 24 hours a day for four days, giving each person a tape recorder and instructions to record all the questions that occurred to him or her requiring an answer from an outside source. They found their subjects had an average of four questions per day, would spend an average of just under nine hours per week searching for answers, and would be willing to pay $14.50 per week to get right answers, up to $10 for answers to important questions and $2 for less important answers. Some said they'd pay $100 or more for answers to critical health questions. Extrapolating roughly, that amounts to about 800 million questions a day for the U.S. adult population and a reservoir of $2.9 billion per week to get those questions answered. Libraries ranked 11th among sources used to answer their questions, at about 4 percent, right between consulting the Yellow Pages and contacting a government agency. (The Internet and search engines came first.) Among the study's conclusions: "Americans have not yet found an ideal information resource. Not one study participant said they would use the same resource time and again when seeking answers."[5]

- According to statistics compiled by the Association of Research Libraries, the median number of reference queries at its 111 member institutions peaked at over 162,000 per year in 1997 and dropped to just under 139,900 in 2001, a decrease of about 14 percent in four years.[6]

So what are we to make of all this? The quick answer is that a lot is changing in the world of information and that a lot isn't. The Internet has rapidly become an important aspect of many people's information world, and this has, I think, also quickly changed the role of information in their lives, how they think about it and, of course, how they will seek it out and use it. We've always known that in most cases, people will exert the least possible effort to find information, unless it is really important to them. For most things, they will ask a friend or colleague, try to find an answer in some personal information system, like their own files or notes, look in a newspaper or other information source at hand, and so on. Only dedicated library users or people who are sufficiently motivated or desperate will turn to a library of some description for help or advice or an answer.

The Internet has now become, for some people in some situations, like asking a friend. In his circuit-court opinion in *ACLU v. Reno*, striking down the Communications Decency Act as unconstitutional, Federal District Judge Stewart Dalzell, seeking an appropriate metaphor for the Internet to decide on how much First Amendment protection it deserved, coined this marvelously descriptive turn of phrase: "Cutting through the acronyms and argot that littered the hearing testimony, the Internet may fairly be regarded as a never-ending worldwide conversation."[7] (I just found this quote by searching Google, by the way—much faster and easier than it would have been any other way.) Part of that conversation has become a way for more people to find more information more quickly from more sources.

Now, consider the typical familiar, traditional library reference service. There's a reference desk staffed with people who understand the resources at hand (at least some of them) and how to search and use them, who know something about the people they're trying to serve (at least some of them), and who are trying to hook up people with appropriate resources to help them with their information needs. Those people have to make contact with this service in some way, either by approaching the desk, calling on the phone, or perhaps writing a letter. This service is centralized by its very nature, and it has to be, not only to take advantage of the information resources at hand but also to efficiently use staff resources. We can easily picture the reference staff, sitting at the desk, sources at the ready, now including a wide variety of high-quality (and quite expensive) licensed digital resources as well as the wonders of the free Internet, waiting for the next patron to approach or perhaps call. And waiting.

The array of resources is much broader, but the picture above is otherwise little different from what one might have seen in a library of 50 years ago or even more. Yet the world in which that library and its reference service operate has radically changed around them. Often, thinking about "What we should do with our reference service?" starts with precisely that—the service. Let's try instead turning the question around, and asking rather, "What should we do for our users?"

PLANNING FOR REFERENCE SERVICES IN A DIGITAL AGE

To do this, we need to become increasingly aware of four key factors that affect our planning: individual users, the communities to which they belong and to which the service is dedicated, where they are, and what they need. Any information need presented to an information service is a product of all four of these, and those characteristics will help to determine how that need can best, if at all, be served. Keep these factors in mind as you read the following examples; I expand on each of them later in this section.

A few examples might help. Let's spin the wheel a few times and see what happens.

1. Someone trying to contact a specific company in Logan, Utah, calls his local public library to ask for the number.[8] Easy—this is ready reference in its purest form, giving a specific answer to a specific question, and as long as the person thinks of calling the library (and has a phone and the number at hand), she or he is all set, assuming there's no deeper, underlying need or question. Any decent reference service could knock this one off in a minute or so, as could 411, or directory assistance, for a small fee, as well as any number of Web sites and perhaps even the company's Web site itself.

2. A college senior wants to write a paper on the change in religion in Restoration England and its relation to Milton's *Samson Agonistes*. He comes to the reference desk of the campus library, approaches the desk, and the librarian gives him some good starting points for his research. Also easy— a deeper, more complicated research question, where the user is present and can take advantage of many different resources, both print and digital, and the librarian can do a bit of teaching on which sources might be good, how to search them, where to go next, and so on. It's harder to imagine where else he might go, though general Web surfing is probably tempting, especially for those last-minute papers and projects. This is where a library reference service shines—past, present, and future.

3. The CEO is in a strategic meeting with her senior executives, and it becomes clear that they need a long-range forecast for consumer adoption of wireless services. Assuming

her corporate library hasn't been eliminated or outsourced, she might choose to assign it the task; she might also turn to a trusted executive whose staff knows the area well and can turn the report around fast. In either case, the wise person responding to this need will move quickly and efficiently and provide the report in an easy-to-understand format with little, if any, "user education" or suggestions for where the user might go next. Although I've put this story in a corporate context, it's easy to imagine the same situation with the mayor, the dean, the principal—whoever the boss is.

4. In a major university library, a person comes to the reference desk of the graduate library and wants to know what percentage of the earth is penguin habitat. The reference librarian's first thought? Exactly: where the heck am I going to find that? After several fruitless attempts using print resources, he wonders whether the Internet would help. A search engine yields a few interesting pages, but what should emerge from the search but a Web page for "Ask a Penguin Expert." (Yes, I made that up, but it wouldn't surprise me.) It looks to be on the level, so the librarian refers the question, and a day or so later the patron gets her answer. Of course, the initial question presented to the librarian was "Do you have any books on the Arctic?" and after a brief but skillful interview process, the real (?) question emerged. It's interesting to ponder what that person would have searched if she had turned first to the Internet, whether she would have found the penguin-expert site, and whether she would then have asked the more specific question directly. The context (organizational, interpersonal, technological, and so on) in which the question is asked may well have a significant effect on the specificity of what's asked—an intriguing notion.

5. A public library in Oregon is just beginning to take reference questions via a form on its Web site. It's a sort of experiment, so the library is not publicizing it much, and a few questions trickle in each day. On the third day, a ques-

tion comes in from someone in the U.K., who found the library's Web site, asking about the history and fate of the Oregon Trail. This question unsettles a couple of staff members. Should we be answering questions via e-mail for people who aren't part of our service population? He's not paying taxes here or supporting the library. Of course, if that person walked in the door or called, his question would be dealt with as would any other, and for many librarians, it would be a novelty and kind of a thrill to help somebody from that far away. Yet the fact that it's come in by e-mail makes it somehow different, at least to some people. Perhaps it's because it took so little effort to ask—he didn't have to come or call—or perhaps it's because the staff is concerned about being overwhelmed by questions from all over the world. From the user's perspective, though, this is a perfect situation: he's found a library that can probably be quite helpful, and that help is a mere mouse click away. The niceties of library funding, institutional responsibility, and so on, are lost on him. It's a *public library*, right?

6. It's 3:15 in the morning, and a graduate student is searching her library's catalog, databases, and Web sites, working on her dissertation. She has some success but gets stuck in some of the finer points of searching and could really use some help. The library building is closed, of course, so she looks through the library's Web site for some way to get assistance while she's searching. She finds a page (after a bit of determined digging) labeled "Ask a Librarian," which at first looks promising but on further investigation is found to say, "Our service goal is to respond to e-mail questions within two to three business days" and will only take "quick, factual questions."[9] It suggests people call or come in for other kinds of questions. This is absolutely unhelpful to her—she needs assistance right now, with the search she's in the middle of, and she has no idea whether her question is quick or not or whether it's factual (as opposed to what?). She appreciates the ability to do her research remotely, es-

pecially since she's doing field study in Japan at the moment, but is frustrated by her inability to get the kind of help she's used to when searching the library in person.

There are, of course, no right or wrong answers to the questions posed here; different libraries and librarians will make different decisions in responding to these kinds of situations and challenges, and this is as it should be. No one-size-fits-all solution is possible or even desirable when it comes to figuring out how each library should construct its services. It would be nice to think that the decisions libraries make are based on deep and reasoned consideration of their users and how best to serve them rather than on how it's always been done, how to respond to yet another round of budget restrictions, and what the reference staff can do and will put up with. Nice, but perhaps unrealistic.

The four factors I was trying to highlight in these little stories are, in my estimation, the most crucial ones in helping libraries think about how to allocate their resources in helping people find information:

- *The individual users*—a question of who they are—students, faculty, staff, alumni, the general public, children, adults, older persons, blind persons, persons wearing uniforms, members of a visible ethnic minority, persons having difficulty communicating in English, senior management, principals
- *The community to which the users belong*—largely a question of whether they "belong" to the library via membership in the geographic or academic or school or corporate or organizational community, but also a question of any affinity that they might have to the library's mission (a visiting lawyer using an out-of-town law library, a local history or genealogy buff, a potential faculty member or student, and so on)
- *Where they are*—a question of whether they are at the reference desk, in the stacks, somewhere on campus, in class, at work, at home, on the street
- *Their information need*—a question of its depth, complexity, subject; how much is wanted; the format in which it is wanted; how quickly an answer is needed

Each library must decide, based on its own unique situation, which of these, individually and in combination, are its highest priorities. Then—most important—it must decide how it should allocate its resources to serve them best, including its most important and most precious resource: its trained staff.

Serving the New 24/7 User

I can't help being drawn back to the final example I presented: the user—regardless of who it is, community, type of library—who is searching a library catalog in the wee, small hours of the morning, plowing through its licensed databases, using its links to interesting, freely available Web sites. What is she doing? She's navigating through information the library owns or has access to or otherwise thinks is worthwhile in much the same way she could while in the library building now or 20 years ago. She's able to do it 24 hours a day from wherever she can get access and authenticate herself, if necessary, and it's a wonderful thing for her to be able to do. On the surface, it's a great service.

Except it isn't. There's one crucial piece missing, one that no librarian would have thought even possible a mere few years ago. She has access to library resources but no access to library services. There is no one for her to ask for help, no librarian, no paraprofessional, no staff, no other patrons, no volunteers—nobody. If anybody had proposed in 1990 that we open up libraries 24 hours a day and leave them unstaffed for half or more of that time, that person would have been scorned, and rightly so. And yet every library that provides access to its catalog and collections via the Web with no capability of asking for help does it every day.

The user we describe here is often called a *remote user*, as though the fact that she is "remote" (that is, not in the building during normal opening hours) means she is somehow different. That sort of distinction is dangerous (and even self-destructive to the future of our profession) because there may well be, now or in the future, many more "remote" users than any other kind, especially as more and more kinds of resources become available in digital and networked formats. And if those users find it difficult to find what they're looking for and they can't ask for help, what do you think they will do?

For all intents and purposes, our user is *in the library;* she is interacting with materials and resources, taking advantage of the library's selection policies, organizational structures, and professional judgment. But it's a thin and pale visit because she is alone, with no one to ask for help, guidance, advice, or even the time. It must be a lonely place for these remote users.

It is simply wrong to provide access without service, and librarians should know better.

In fact, there's an argument to be made that people bouncing around the Web site at 3:15 in the morning are deserving of even *more* service than those who are there at noon. If they are in the same time zone as the library itself, they're likely in pretty desperate straits, searching for something they're really interested in, in the middle of the night. This might be the only time of day in which they can interact with the library because of work or family or other obligations. Perhaps they're just bored or insomniacs and idly surfing. For people in other time zones, if they've found their way to the Web site of a library halfway around the world, there might be something they think they'll find there that they won't find anywhere else. In any of these circumstances, these people seem, to me at least, to be pretty good candidates for the kind of personalized service librarians justifiably pride themselves on.

There are a number of classes of users who could receive superior service via some technological or digital means. In an academic setting, consider students in distance-education programs or otherwise studying remotely, faculty who work at home, alumni, potential students or faculty, and other people who need information about the institution. In the public library, there are members of the community who are homebound, temporarily out of the geographic area, or at work during library opening hours. In a corporate or organizational context, if sufficiently far-flung, people around the city, region, country, or world could be served well by a networked service. And in any context, services could target users who have limited or no visual, auditory, or vocal abilities or who have mobility impairments or who speak many languages other than English.

There is also another intriguing possibility here. It is possible that developing, implementing, and publicizing services that take advantage of digital and networked technologies will encourage use by people we don't often see. It might just be the case that these services will bring out more, say, people from the so-called generation X, teenagers or college students using cell phones, the business community, or other people who don't currently think of "the library" (by which they mean the building with books in it for kids to read) as a place where they can get help, information, guidance, and so on. That would be terrific, of course, for any library, but this might also raise even more difficult questions about reallocation of resources, how services are designed, what the core mission of the library is, and the like. One would assume that our core values persist, but this might be a fun challenge and thought experiment to take on.

THE CHANGING ROLE OF THE REFERENCE INTERVIEW

To be able to respond to any individual's information need, it is of course necessary to find out what it is. In the world of reference we've all been familiar with, this is accomplished via the reference interview. Much has been written about reference interviews—how to conduct them, what their objectives are, and so on.

All of this practice and experience, however, makes one crucial assumption: that the person with the information need is there to be interviewed, either on the phone or in person. To be sure, correspondence reference conducted via mail has been around for quite a while, but it has always occupied a tiny fraction of reference for the large majority of libraries. What can be done to replicate the objectives, if not the practice, of the reference interview in a digital environment? The following sections discuss the role of the reference interview in a digital world, options for soliciting information needs, and issues raised.

The Synchronous Reference Interview

Well, to begin with, this is a misnomer, because in most settings there won't really be anything that closely resembles the reference interview most of us are familiar with. It may even be a mistake to think of it this way, but let's start with this and see where it leads us.

We first must look at the two possible ways in which this transaction may be handled. Either it goes on in a synchronous way, via some real-time mechanism such as chat, instant messaging, videoconferencing, and so on, or it will be asynchronous, using e-mail, Web forms, bulletin boards, and the like. These are two quite different ways of going about things and thus should be examined separately.

In synchronous modes, the give-and-take aspect of the familiar reference interview is, or can be, largely preserved. I think this is one of the reasons many people think that reference using these technologies would be preferable to asynchronous methods, and there may be something to that argument. Certainly, it would be easier in some ways to build on the body of experience and expertise among reference professionals by more closely mimicking the ways in which they are already accustomed to interacting with people. It may well be that traditional reference-interview skills and procedures will translate well into this synchronous world. At this point, the jury's still out on that one, since only a small but growing number of libraries and organizations have experimented with doing reference this way.

I have to admit to a bit of skepticism about all of this. I think there may well be merit in the notion that a real-time interaction is better for some kinds of people with some kinds of needs and questions and for some kinds of services. But I have difficulty imagining people without experience with these kinds of technologies embracing them simply for this. And while there are groups of people for whom chat and instant messaging are second nature (especially among the young), these pale in comparison to the number of people who are comfortable with, or at least able to use, e-mail or who can fill in a Web form. And at this stage, the early anecdotal evidence, on chat-based services at least, is that they are underutilized.

I could be completely wrong about this: synchronous digital reference could well be the best way to go for a large number of people and communities and their needs, and it's simply a matter of waiting for the right technology or for that technology to be widely used. Perhaps services based on wireless devices, personal digital assistants, cell phones, and their descendants will be the key. But at the moment, I don't think that is the answer . . . yet.

The Asynchronous Reference Interview

So let me focus here on asynchronous services, which we have a great deal more (although still limited) experience with. Here, the primary reason it might be wrong to think of soliciting information needs in a digital world as a reference interview is that it will likely lack the back-and-forth of the interview. It may well be a one-shot deal, and that's not necessarily a bad thing.

This idea flips out a lot of reference librarians who are used to having the ability to ask lots of questions and to make sure that they get the nuance of the user's information need, who are able to find out whether there is more (or less) going on beneath the surface, and most important, feel confident that their interviewing skills will guarantee that they're answering the right question. I have to admit there's a lot to that argument, but I'm not sure it holds much water. We all know that there are users who are unwilling—or unable—to tell us what they really want. The young woman who asked me where the collection of standardized tests was (when she really wanted a copy of Beck's depression inventory, which we found on the Internet) and the gentleman who asked for directions to the cookbooks (when he really wanted typical menus for several different countries and recipes for making the dishes) are fairly typical examples of what I call the "do you have any books on fish?" effect.

You know that effect, I'm sure only too well. I tell my students that the first two utterances of any reference interview are essentially content free. Like this:

> **Librarian:** Good morning! May I help you? [*Translation:* I am here to help you.]
> **Library user:** Yes. Do you have any books on fish? [*Translation:* I understand that you are here to help me, and I need that help.]

Very little information has changed hands here. It's almost like establishing a telecommunications link via a network or modem; it feels much more like making a connection, agreeing on protocols, and so on, than a conversation. Once this connection is developed, then the interview can actually begin:

> **Librarian:** Sure. Are you looking for anything specific? [*Translation:* Which of the many thousands of possible things about fish, if any, do you really want to know more about?]
> **Library user:** Um, yeah. Can you help me find out what fish live in the Mississippi River? [*Translation:* It would have felt weird for me to just blurt that out right away, and besides I knew you'd ask me for more, so I'll tell you what I really want now, but I won't tell you everything or ask too much because I don't want to look stupid.]

The interview isn't over yet; the librarian still has to find out a few more things, like what, if anything, he's already looked through, how much information he wants, what he's going to use it for (a very tricky but vital question to ask), and so on. She'll do all of this fairly quickly, and of course *she* doesn't want to look stupid either, so she's rolling through lots of possible sources and search strategies in her mind, deciding whether to start with the library catalog, the Web, a standard reference resource, a referral, and so on, while still trying to keep the user engaged and move it along. It's an exhausting proposition, and good reference librarians make it look very easy.

I've certainly worked with people who felt quite comfortable telling me their life stories, including lots of good background on their question but also more than I wanted or needed to know. But I've also had questioners who were very reluctant, for whatever reason, to tell me much more than the basic subject area of their question.

One of the key issues here is that both people realize that this is, at least at some level, an interactive process, so it's OK to hold things back, keep trying to find out more, and so on. It's partially a conversation and thus is subject to some of the norms of social interaction, and it's nigh impossible to extract it from its social context. The reference interview is the way it is in no small part because it's the product of two people talking to each other.

Today's Reference "Noninterview"

But what if it isn't like that anymore? What if it becomes possible to accomplish some of the same goals outside that social context, by using e-mail or Web forms to find out what people want to know? Then it really isn't an interview anymore, really, and it's more than likely a one-shot deal. And the technologies we're using in large part reinforce that idea. When sending an e-mail question to a library reference service or filling out a Web form, I think most people assume that's it and that an answer will come back rather than more questions. So the first thing we get is likely all we might get and, therefore, all we will have to go on to make an intelligent response.

And this is the part that unnerves a lot of good reference librarians. My research (Janes, 2001) has shown that up to half of digital reference services are emphasizing quick, factual, ready-reference-type questions over more detailed research, source-recommendation questions, to the point of putting sometimes extensive policy statements on their sites. For example, I've seen a form that tells potential inquirers that they should ask "questions you might ask at the reference desk of any public library," which wouldn't be of much help to people who don't ask questions at public library reference desks. Another one says that it won't answer "trivia questions" but doesn't explain what it means by that, leaving one to wonder what would happen if a "trivia" question came to the desk or the phone.

I've also seen one that says, "This service is best used for questions that library staff can research and answer without further input from you. Some questions are complex and require discussion with our staff and/or a visit to the library." I think I know what they're going for here—they're trying not to promise the world or raise expectations they can't fulfill, and they're simultaneously trying to guide people to ask questions that can be successfully answered via these technologies. All of these are laudable goals, and they're on the right track, but I also think that language isn't necessarily helpful to most nonlibrarians, because they're probably not very good judges of what questions are and aren't complex and would require further input or discussion with staff. Right idea—needs just a bit more work. More on this in Chapter 6.

I've also found that reference librarians very strongly feel that digital reference in general is far better for ready-reference questions than for research questions. I think that a goodly part of this deeply held belief is based on this notion that it's impossible to do a proper interview in this environment and therefore all we can hope for is to get quick factual-type questions, where the interview is less important or necessary, and leave the deeper questions for in-person work, where we can really find out what the users want and help them to find it.

That's a great idea, and it's wrong. I'm going to echo my colleague Sara Weissman of the Morris County Public Library in New Jersey, who's been doing reference for a long time and doing digital reference in lots of ways (including moderating chat groups in America Online) for a long time. She said something to me in a conversation that has stayed with me ever since: the reference interview is overrated.

What a bolt that was. What heresy! The reference interview, keystone to a successful reference interaction and linchpin of the profession—overrated? Get out the pitchforks and torches!

Here's what she really said: when people are asking for help, they will tell whoever is offering the help only about as much as they want that person to know and not much more. That's why some reference interviews feel like pulling teeth and why in others a reference librarian knows that there is more going on beneath the surface that she or he never got at. Of course not—they have no intention of telling you what their deep motivation is because they don't think it's any of your business or they're embarrassed or scared or nervous and they just want some help to move forward in finding out whatever it is that they want to know. Certainly, good reference librarians need to clarify the question as best they can, make sure they're in the right area, and get all the background and contextual information they can. But that should be it. If patrons only want to tell you a little bit of what's really going on, they can't (and perhaps don't?) expect to get a fully featured, complete, and comprehensive "answer." They're going to get moved forward, so guiding them to a potentially good source or two or to the general area in the stacks where their subject is or giving them a subject heading you think would be helpful is about as good as it's going to get. And no more.

So people who ask sketchy questions get sketchy responses, and people who are willing to spill their guts get more. Sara called this answering their questions at their own level, and I think she's absolutely right. With luck, if we do a good job and respect their privacy and unwillingness to tell us everything, they'll come back if they need more or aren't finding what they need. If not, I still think that repeatedly asking people questions they're demonstrably unwilling to answer is just a bad idea, not to mention largely ineffective. Once in a while, you might be able to get more, but I'm not sure it's worth it if you take the larger view.

I am not, however, suggesting we abandon the reference interview, either in person or digitally. Quite the reverse. I'm going to claim that in some circumstances you can do a much better, more efficient, and more effective job of finding out what people really want to know using digital reference techniques than you can in person. We'll revisit this point shortly.

In the meantime, let's look at ways in which it might be possible to use digital technologies to find out about people's information needs.

ASYNCHRONOUS REFERENCE SERVICE MODELS

Most reference librarians are used to and comfortable with two primary ways of working with information needs in the form of the familiar reference interview: either in person or over the telephone. Both, of necessity, require the questioners to present themselves at a time and day when the library is open, or at least when a service is staffed (in the case, for example, of a telephone-only service). This sort of exchange happens in real time and involves direct, synchronous communication between them.

As with the reference interviews I discussed earlier, in the digital realm the two primary modes for soliciting information needs are synchronous and asynchronous. We'll deal with the asynchronous types here and leave the discussion of synchronous (chat-, voice-over-IP-, instant-messaging-, and call-center-based systems) for Chapter 4, when we talk about technologies.

Asynchronous reference really isn't all that different from correspondence reference, which arose and became commonplace in the late nineteenth century, at least among research libraries. It is interesting to note that Ryan is able to cite only a handful of items from the professional (and none from the scholarly) literature on correspondence reference (1996). Rothstein says that in the late 1800s, "[n]early all the general research libraries professed surprising willingness to go to considerable lengths in answering mail inquiries" (1955: 55), Levin comments that "[r]eference work by correspondence is a branch of library service which seems to remain a virgin field" (1947: 603–604), and a committee of the Association of College and Research Libraries lists a series of types of questions that libraries should not refer to other libraries when received in the mail, including requests from its own patrons, unless their facilities are inadequate, requests that library itself is uniquely or best able to answer, medical and legal questions, and "[r]equests that cannot be deciphered or are so vague that it would be impossible to answer them without clarification" (1952: 3–4).

Indeed, the two major textbooks of reference of the early twentieth century, those of Wyer (1930) and Hutchins (1944), are nearly silent on correspondence reference, both addressing it under the heading of "administration." Wyer's mention is oblique at best; Hutchins spends her paragraph on this topic suggesting that requests from patrons be referred to the library in their city, unless they claim their own library can't help them and they know yours can, in which case they "should be helped." She suggests that librarians should be the ones referring questions by mail, to get the benefit of the reference interview and any previous searching, and suggests some libraries adopted fees to reduce the volume of correspondence reference requests (1944: 173). Hardly what we might consider a user-centered approach today, but this mind-set likely differs little from current practice, at least in some libraries.

E-mail and Web Forms

In the digital environment, asynchronous reference exchanges typically go on via electronic mail, although a few Web-based bulletin-board systems have been tried. Patrons send in their questions via e-mail or a Web form maintained by the library.

An exclusively e-mail-based system is attractive, especially for smaller libraries or those with limited technological resources or experience. It requires little beyond setting up an e-mail account or using an existing one, either on the library's server or with a free e-mail service, such as Hotmail or Yahoo! mail. Adding a mailto tag and link on the library's Web site or even just publicizing an e-mail address begins to inform the community that reference questions can be sent in this way. In fact, in many cases, librarians report that their users were there first: they began receiving reference questions in e-mail accounts for general information, addressed to the library Webmaster, or for other purposes. Somebody sends an e-mail message with the question, it is received by the library (more on this shortly), and some time later an e-mail message with a response is sent back. Simple, quick, and in some cases perfectly reasonable.

A step up, at least technologically, is the use of a Web form. Somewhere on the library's Web site, users find a form to fill in, indicating their question. (Again, in some places, patrons were ahead of the game, using other forms for comments, complaints, suggestions, and so on to submit questions on.) That form almost always asks for a few basic pieces of information, such as the user's e-mail address and name and question. Simple forms such as these are quick and easy to construct and may appear attractive and easy to fill for the user.

The use of e-mail and simple forms, though, really only resembles the opening refrains of the reference interview. They solicit very little information and perhaps even dictate sketchy inquiries from users. If we truly want to take advantage of our collective experience in reference practice, perhaps it is best to invest forms with what we know about questions that really help in determining what a person wants to know and that help us find ways to assist.

First, here's an example of an actual Internet Public Library (IPL) question that came to an e-mail address:

```
From: @aol.com
Date: Tue, 26 Jun 2001 13:39:07 EDT
Subject: Values
To: ipl@ipl.org
MIME-Version: 1.0
Content-Type: text/plain; charset="US-ASCII"
Content-Transfer-Encoding: 7bit
X-Mailer: AOL 5.0 for Windows sub 124
What do I hit to find prices/values on old magazines? First
issues, etc.
```

Figure 2.1 Sample E-mail Reference Question.

It wouldn't be hard to construct a meaningful response to a question such as this, but it leaves a lot to be desired, and there are many ways it could go. How old are these magazines? Are you interested in specific ones? Are you trying to sell or buy? Where are you? (And what exactly does "What do I hit" refer to, anyway?)

Question:
I'm interested in a career as a Spanish/English translator. I'm not biligual and need to learn Spanish. What I need to know is where to get the education in an imersion form. Also, and more importantly, is there a need for translators, can one make a good living in this field, and is there a particular niche (eg medical/legal) which is more likely to garner work?

area: Education
reason: I'm looking for a career change, and have always wanted to be bilingual.
school: No
answer_type: sources
format3: doesn't matter

Question:
I am interested in the African country Burundi as part of the African Great Lakes area. Its geography, history and politics. I am particularly interested in analyses of the ethnic composition of its population and the nature of the relationships between them—from land ownership and tenure systems, ownership of cattle and relationships based on gifts of cattle from the tutsi to the hutus and the resulting tributary relationship between the donor and the recipient.

Annotated bibliographic material would be most gratefully received and acknowledged.

location: Tanzania
area: History
reason: I am writing a paper which is intended to help people understand the origins of the crisis that has claimed hundreds of thousands of lives in that country in periodic blood letting. I am a publisher in Tanzania but have also been on the Nyerere's team and after him Mandela's facilitating negotiations between the different political partied in that country. The negotiations which have been taking place in the town of Arusha Tanzania have officially come to an end but the problem is nowhere near solution.
school: Yes
answer_type: sources
format1: internet sources
format2: print sources
format3: doesn't matter
sources_consulted: Encyclopaedia Brittanica, Encarta. Have collected a of books and what to see what there is that I have not seen that could be of use.

Figure 2.2 Sample Form-Based Digital Reference Inquiries.

Hi,
When I was about 11 years old 1969 I read a book. It was about a group of people crossing the mountains to get to California. It was near winter and Indians came(I think they were blackfeet) and killed all of the adults and destroyed the wagons etc. All of the children had been hidden and were left to fend for themselves after the Indians had gone. The oldest of them was a girl named Laurie. She was about 15(I think). At the end of the book they were rescued and taken to a military fort. This is all I know of the book. I don't remember the name or author. How in the world do I find this book. I can still remember reading it and would love to read it to my grandaughter. Can anyone help me?

location: Clarkston,MI U.S.A.
area: Literature
reason: I homeschool my grandchildren and would love to share this great book with them.
school: Yes
answer_type: sources
format3: doesn't matter
sources_consulted: I typed in blackfee and Laurie in my search but didn't find anything. Since I don't know the name of the book I am kind of lost.

Figure 2.2 Continued

Figure 2.2 shows a couple of examples that illustrate what kinds of things can emerge from Web-form interviews. The questions all came in to the reference service of the IPL, www.ipl.org, via its Web reference form (the one shown in Figure 2.1 came in through its e-mail address and thus didn't use the form). That form can be found at http://www.ipl.org/div/askus/refformqrc.html and has been revised on several occasions since the IPL opened in 1995, based on IPL staff and student experience in answering over 30,000 questions via digital reference. It's on the following page as Figure 2.3.

Aside from being fascinating questions in their own right, these are illustrations of a phenomenon we haven't seen much for a while, since the days when correspondence or reference was common. It's not difficult for an experienced reference librarian to imagine how interactions with these people would begin if they presented themselves at a reference desk or called on the phone. "Do you have any information on Burundi?" or "on Africa?" "Where are your Spanish books?" "I'm looking for a book I read as a girl."

IPL Ask A Question Form

PLEASE READ!

Before you ask a question, please read this informational page about our service. If you are under the age of 13, please use the KidSpace Ask a Question service.

---

1 **What is your name?**

What is your email address?

If you don't give us your correct, complete e-mail (example: fluggly@aol.com), we can't send you an answer to your question. **AOL users:** If you have parental or mail controls turned on, add iplref@ipl.org to your allowed mail list so we can send you e-mail!

Where do you live? (City/State/ Country)

We can usually help you better if we know where you live, and how far away you are from the resources we may recommend to you.

---

2 **I won't need this information after:** _____ (mm/dd/yy)

If you need an answer in less than 3 days, we are not the service for you. Click here for other suggestions.

---

3 **The Subject Area of the Question:** (click to see list -- choose one)

[(None Selected) ▼]

---

4 **Please tell us your question.**

A human being will read your question -- please use complete sentences! The more you tell us, the better our answer will be. What do you already know about your subject or question?

---

5 **How will you use this information?** Why are you asking your question? If you're just curious, that's ok, but it really helps librarians to know this part! Sometimes we can use our subject knowledge and imaginations to think of other places to look for answers and information, if we know how you will use it or what you want to get out of the answer.

Will you use this information for a school assignment? ○ Yes ○ No
Are you: ☐ A librarian? ☐ A teacher? ☐ A businessperson?

---

6 **Type of answer preferred:** (choose one of the following)

○ A brief factual answer to your question
○ Some ideas for sources to consult for exploration:

☐ Internet sources ☐ Print sources ☐ I don't care which kind

Sometimes the information you want isn't available on the Internet, but might be available through a library near you. We can almost always get you started, at least.

---

7 **Sources Consulted:**

Please list any places on the Net or off that you've already checked regarding your question. We don't want to duplicate your attempts. Don't forget to try using our Subject Collections and your local library to answer your question.

---

8 **SEND IT!**

Reminder: Please take a moment to re-check the e-mail address you are submitting to us, since it is **impossible** for us to communicate with you unless it is correct. Also, if you have not read our Privacy Statement, please do so. Thanks!

Please confirm your email address. _____

[Submit Question] [Clear Form]

Figure 2.3 IPL Reference-Question Form.

Good reference librarians, of course, will probe those opening salvos and find out more about what the patrons really want, how they will use the information, how much they want, the formats, and so on. A well-crafted Web reference form can accomplish much of the same and has a few side benefits as well.

(A quick note on the IPL: it started as a class project in a graduate seminar I taught in 1995 at the then School of Information and Library Studies at the University of Michigan. After the class ended, the IPL continued and now is an education project of the School of Information at Michigan. I served as the director of the IPL for several years, and though I currently don't have any formal role with it, I still refer to the people who work there as "we," so I'll continue that here. To learn more about the IPL, its work and lessons, I recommend *The Internet Public Library Handbook*[10] and other popular and scholarly pieces listed on the IPL's Web site.[11])

This form is among the best examples I know of, although admittedly I'm biased, and although the form itself is quite involved, it provides users with a number of ways to express their needs in a complete and thorough fashion. It's certainly not perfect and certainly not the only or best answer for any other setting, but it does give some idea of what may be possible using a form.

In each of these cases, the questioners have had the opportunity to compose their information needs in a coherent way and in the process have given us a significant amount of information about those needs. I like to think of this as scaffolding the inquiry, giving users a level of support in framing and expressing their needs in a way that can not only help a librarian to find appropriate resources but also help the users themselves better understand and focus their questions.

Digital reference forms such as these (and, in fact, digital reference in general) are of great use to people with complicated information needs or questions. In a traditional, face-to-face interview, it can be difficult to either get people to convey the full complexity of their needs or make sense of it from the mad rush (what I often call the "confessional barf") of information—previous searches, what they will use the information for, how much they want, and so on. That torrent can often be helpful, but it's often disorganized, and the librarian is usually contemplating sources and strategies before it all comes out.

Contrast that with the use of this form. The users above were able to look at this form, study it, and use it to structure their inquiries. (Do they always do that and thus provide beautifully structured questions, models of coherence and clarity? Yeah, right.) In an ideal universe, they then could respond to each of the individual questions in turn, providing an excellent foundation for the librarian. In practice, one often sees the phenomenon illustrated by the first two questions, where the users are almost interviewing themselves, and successively more specific (and informative) levels of the information needs are revealed sentence by sentence. Subsequent requests for type of answer preferred and sources consulted also at times provide new and quite helpful tidbits for the responder.

Asking Why

I have always thought, though, that it's much easier to ask the *why* question in this environment—partially because of human nature and partially because of people's images of librarians. But I think it's very hard for most librarians to ask the "Why do you want to know this?" question without coming off like a *librarian*, glasses firmly perched on the end of the nose (even if you're not wearing glasses), asking, "Why do you want to know this?," lips pursed, hair firmly pulled back into the stereotypical librarian bun, vaguely disapproving expression on the face—the whole bit. This might be why some librarians find the questions difficult to ask and perhaps even why some people don't ask librarians—for fear of having to answer it. Dervin and Dewdney, attempting to link reference practice to Dervin's theory of sense making as a model for information-seeking behavior, suggest using neutral questions to get people to talk about their intended uses for information:

- How are you planning to use this information?
- If you could have exactly the help you wanted, what would it be?

- How will this help you? What will it help you do?
- If you could tell me the kind of problem you're working on, I'll have a better idea of what would help you. (1986: 509, 510)

I happen to think they're right, but even they admit that many librarians, in workshops teaching neutral questioning techniques, found them "'odd,' 'unnatural,' or 'awkward'" or only useful "when the user was having obvious and extreme difficulties articulating the information need" (1986: 511).

The language in questions 4 and 5 on the IPL reference-question form is an attempt to get those questions stated in a coherent fashion. It's not just users who need help in organizing their thoughts—those questions can be as difficult to ask as they are to answer. There's a lot of information and a lot going on in those questions, and using a Web form to ask them and to allow people to construct answers to them *in their own time* avoids the tensions inherent in the interpersonal aspect of a face-to-face or phone interview. The form is asking potential users to help the librarians to help them by providing as much context and background as they are comfortable with. The enforced anonymity (or at least facelessness) of the form also might help with potentially very personal, private, or embarrassing inquiries.

Limitations of Web Forms

There are a couple of important criticisms, or at least questions, about all of this, and they demand to be taken seriously. The most serious is that so many aspects of what we're used to in the reference interview are missing here: the opportunity for give and take, discussion, and interactivity; the relatively low bandwidth of the conversation; the lack of body language, vocal intonation, and so on—not to mention the simple human connection made between two people in a setting such as this. It's true—most of that is gone here. It might be possible to respond with an e-mail to clarify when necessary, but that will likely take a long time, and multiple volleys would be impossible or incredibly time-consuming, not to mention tedious.

And the body language and vocal intonation are indeed gone; it's amazing how quickly people substitute spelling, typing, grammar, e-mail domain, and so on for those kinds of nonverbal aspects of the interview, however, to help fill in the gaps. Instead of stereotyping people based on age or ethnicity or aroma or dress or perceived status, we can now stereotype them based on their CAPITALIZING EVERY WORD IN THE QUESTION or their aol.com versus .edu or .hk. (In chat-based services, perhaps we'll start to judge people by typing speed as well as accuracy.) Some of those aspects can be as useful as what we can glean from nonverbal in-person features but are quite different in many ways.

So is body language necessary to do reference? Clearly not, because we do phone and mail-based reference all the time and have for decades. Does it make a significant difference? I don't know of any evidence that in-person services are more accurate or highly rated than phone services—or e-mail-based services, for that matter. It would appear, then, that body language is simply something we're used to and like, but the lack of it doesn't mean we can't do a reasonably good job in helping people find things that would be of use or interest to them. And if we were being honest, we'd admit that sometimes, at least, that body language and those stereotypes get in the way. It is hard not to give people a different kind of service if they're slouching on the desk, if they smell bad, if they seem threatening or disinterested, or if they seem out of place. I know good librarians do their best to not let that get in the way and it's that kind of professionalism that makes me think we can similarly overcome typing and spelling and domain names in the digital domain.

Another criticism I've heard, especially of detailed forms such as the IPL's, is that they're *too* detailed, that people may be intimidated by them and thus not use the service because the form looks too—well—formidable. I can certainly imagine this might be the case for certain classes of people or perhaps for certain communities (those not facile with English or who are inherently suspicious of Web forms asking for too much information in an increasingly privacy-conscious Web) or for certain questions. If this is the case—and this is an intriguing question for empirical investigation—then it would be wise for libraries to offer multiple faces to their services, as they already do, allowing people to submit simpler forms or e-mail messages (note the statement on e-mail at the bottom of the IPL form), call, visit, chat, and so on. As I've said, with this as with so much else in the evolving reference world, your mileage may vary.

These forms are best if they take the tack of how to help them to help you to help them. People who approach libraries for help are expecting a certain amount of give and take or to be asked to explain what they want (or at least most of them are), and so they're probably willing to go along with whatever methods seem reasonable and necessary to get them the help they're looking for.

Design Considerations for Web-Based Forms

We've discussed a few of these already. It's important to ask, of course, for *e-mail address,* what the *question* is, what *sources* they've consulted, and what they might *use the information for.* Let's walk first through the IPL form and touch on a few other items there and also discuss other questions librarians might want to consider including.

In section 1, there's a question on *location* (here, city, state, and country). That might be worth asking, not only to authenticate whether the person is a library patron (that is, part of the service population) but also to determine how close the user is to a branch, if the user is a distance-education student or employee in another office or division, and so on. Similarly, you might want to ask for a phone number, fax number, mailing address (if you also ask how the user wants to get the response).

It might also be wise or necessary to ask for explicit *authentication* via means such as student number, library-card number, phone number, password, PIN, and so on. If a library's policies dictate that it will only respond to inquiries from people who are part of a service population, such authentication makes sense. It might even be required for the use of licensed databases or other resources.

IPL also asks for the *name.* It's asked so that the librarian can make that extra little connection with the questioner. When the response goes back, the person answering almost always includes a short greeting using the questioner's name, if it's known. A small touch, to be sure, but perhaps a nice one, justifying asking the question, which of course people are free to ignore or fabricate a response to.

Question 2 asks for a *date* by which the information is needed. This is often a good idea and gives the answerer a sense of urgency and how much time he or she has to respond. IPL, as a volunteer-based and experimental service, can't guarantee much more than a three-day turnaround, but other libraries will likely be able to do better. (More on policies such as these later.) It would be good, though, to reemphasize that in this kind of service, an immediate answer is unlikely, but a quick one might be forthcoming.

Question 3 provides a list of 20 or so *broad categories* for people to assign to their question to help in the answering process. In practice, research shows that the most often selected category is "Other/Misc" (Carter and Janes, 2000), which isn't even the default. More than four out of ten users submitting a form select that choice, dwarfing all other category choices. The lesson here is that people have a difficult time with even that broad-level categorization of their need, and we shouldn't expect much more from them. In fact, in its early days, the IPL form asked people to suggest *keywords* for their questions, but this is no longer asked. Most people simply couldn't do it, and asking for keywords just reinforced for some people that what they typed into these boxes was going to a search engine rather than a person. See the language in question 4, an attempt to get them to tell us whatever they know, or don't know, about their information need.

Question 5 includes not only the now infamous *why* question but also some simple *demographic* questions. The IPL asks these to help in framing responses (for example, to other librarians, we can use jargon such as OCLC and Dialog that laypeople don't need to hear). In other settings, asking about *status* (student/staff/faculty) might make sense, as would questions about *age, grade level,* and the like.

Question 6 gives people a chance to specify desired *characteristics* of the response. IPL's research has found that people have difficulty here. When the questions are received, they are processed by professionals and senior students and, as part of that process, assigned to one of two internal categories, one for factual questions and one for sources-type questions, and these administrators have the option of overriding the users' indications when submitting the form, based on their experience and what kind of answer they think would be best. When people indicate they want sources, the administrators place the question in the factual category 6 percent of the time; when people indicate they want a factual answer, they are overridden 40 percent of the time. Either the IPL administrators are arrogant and overreaching or people are poor judges of this aspect of the nature of their needs. The question is still worth asking (and the questioner's original decision is preserved in the result of the form, which answerers see), as is the following question on the *nature* of the sources desired, but probably shouldn't be accepted without question or at least review.

Question 7 asks for *sources* the user may already have consulted. Responses here range, as might be expected, from absolutely nothing to quite sophisticated searches and strategies, especially in questions submitted from other librarians. In some cases, this question also produces more of the need as well.

Question 8 betrays a common problem. It's hard to answer an e-mail question without a correct e-mail address to respond to, and it's extremely frustrating to compose a beautifully thought-through answer only to have it bounce back at you because someone mistyped or misremembered her or his e-mail address. The form asks for confirmation to help to avoid this problem; it certainly doesn't eliminate people who correctly type an invalid address twice, but it does help.

Asynchronous Interactivity

Even though we're discussing asynchronous approaches here, I don't want to completely dismiss the notion of *interactivity* in this domain. I've always wondered if it might be possible to use a series of forms with just a few questions on them, smaller than the long IPL form but more substantial than the name-address-question type but with different second or third forms presented to the questioners based on their answers to the first. For example, on the first form, you might ask about when they need the answer by. They submit that form, and if their deadline is really quick, the second form might tell them that they can only expect a quick answer to certain kinds of questions or that the answer might be pretty cursory to meet their deadline if it's an involved question. Or you might ask whether they prefer Internet or print sources and then ask more detailed questions on the type of source and depth of information after that. I don't know of anybody who's done this, and it's probably much more complicated than it sounds, but it's an intriguing idea nonetheless.

Ten Questions We Get All The Time

What are the Seven Wonders of the Ancient World? What about the Natural Wonders? Modern Wonders? etc.

I've heard there are only 7 (or 5, 20, 36, 37 . . .) basic plots (or themes) in all of literature. What are they?

How do I cite a website in my research paper bibliography?

How much is my 1983 Ford Fiesta worth now?

What were the names of everyone on the Mayflower?

What is an appropriate gift for a couple's silver anniversary?

Where can I get help with my math homework?

There are three words in the English language that end in -gry. Angry and hungry are two of them, what is the third?

Why is the sky blue?

Can you help me find a song/poem/story my grandmother used to read to me when I was a child?

Figure 2.4 IPL's FAQ. From Internet Public Library, "You Are Not Alone (Maybe)." Available at: www.ipl.org/div/farq/.

It's pretty clear that there are certain kinds of users in certain kinds of communities with certain kinds of information needs that are really inappropriate for this sort of service: people with no or limited access to technology or e-mail, people unable to type or to have someone else type for them, people who are uncomfortable with technology or just prefer to interact with another person, people who need an immediate answer, inquiries that require the kind of detailed, interactive reference interview we're accustomed to. For those people, communities, and needs, other services—in person, over the phone, community-information resources, the bookmobile or other outreach services—will certainly be necessary and appropriate. But finding the right mix of all these kinds of services should be the goal for any library to best serve its communities.

QUESTIONS FOR REVIEW

- More than once, I've heard the "who needs the library—everything's on the Web?" argument. What should be our calm, considered, professional response to this nonsense?
- On page 46, I say that that user is "in the library" when using Web-based materials in the middle of the night. This begs important questions: what *is* "the library," and what are its *boundaries,* if they are not the physical walls?
- Can you imagine a technologically mediated reference-interview environment that preserves all the positive aspects of the face-to-face interview and yet permits it to be done at the time and point of need? What technologies would need to be developed or adapted to make that happen? And how would our training and attitudes have to change?
- And if such a thing can't be built, push is eventually going to come to shove. Which is more important, our ability to do a proper, fully featured reference interview or the user's ability to get at us at the time and point of need? Does one of these trump the other?

- For the environments you know well, how many questions would be too many on a Web-based interview form?
- Almost every reference form I've ever seen asks for the questioner's name, IPL's included. It does permit a nice, personalized response. But in an increasingly privacy-focused and even paranoid world, is it still a good idea?

ENDNOTES

1. George D'Elia, Corinne Jorgensen, and Joseph Woelfel, "The Impact of the Internet on Public Library Use: An Analysis of the Current Consumer Market for Library and Information Services." Urban Libraries Council, Evanston, Ill., 2000. Available at: www.urbanlibraries.org/pdfs/finalulc.pdf.
2. U.S. Security and Exchange Commission, Form 10-K/A for Ask Jeeves, Inc., for fiscal year ended December 31, 2000. Available at: www.sec.gov/Archives/edgar/data/1054298/000091205701518994/0000912057–01–518994-index.htm.
3. Danny Sullivan, "Searches per Day," *SearchEngineWatch.com.* Available at: www.searchenginewatch.com/reports/perday.html.
4. U.S. Security and Exchange Commission, Form 10-K for Yahoo!, Inc., for fiscal year ended December 31, 2000. Available at: www.sec.gov/Archives/edgar/data/1011006/000091205701007693/a2041586z10-k.htm.
5. Keen.com and Lewis, Mobilio & Associates, "Consumer Daily Question Study: Summary." Available at: www.keen.com/documents/corpinfo/pressstudy.asp.
6. Information generated from statistics at Association of Research Libraries, University of Virginia Library, "ARL Statistics," interactive edition. Available at: http://fisher.lib.virginia.edu/arl/index.html.
7. *ACLU v. Reno,* 929 F. Supp. 834, 830–49 (ED Pa. 1996).
8. Wherever possible, reference questions and war stories such as these are real, either real questions I've worked with or stories from friends and colleagues. Identifying information, if any, has been changed to protect questioners' confidentiality and privacy.
9. These are both direct quotations from library digital reference Web sites and are fairly typical, based on my research. Some are better, some are worse.
10. Joseph Janes et al., ed., *The Internet Public Library Handbook* (New York: Neal-Schuman, 1999).
11. Internet Public Library, "IPL Press Clippings Bibliography." Available at: www.ipl.org/div/about/press/.

REFERENCES

Association of College and Research Libraries. 1952. *Report of the Committee for the Referral of Reference Inquiries.* Chicago: Association of College and Research Libraries.

Carter, David, and Joseph Janes. 2000. "Unobtrusive Data Analysis of Digital Reference Questions and Service at the Internet Public Library: An Exploratory Study." *Library Trends* 49, no. 2 (fall): 251–65.

Dervin, Brenda, and Patricia Dewdney. 1986. "Neutral Questioning: A New Approach to the Reference Interview." *Reference Quarterly* 25, no. 4 (summer): 506–13.

Hutchins, Margaret. 1944. *Introduction to Reference Work.* Chicago: American Library Association.

Janes, Joseph. 2001. "Digital Reference Services in Public and Academic Libraries." In *Evaluating Networked Information Services: Techniques, Policy and Issues,* edited by Charles McClure and John Carlo Bertot. ASIST Monograph. Medford, N.J.: Information Today.

Levin, Selma. 1947. "Reference Work by Mail Order: A Day in the Life of a Branch Reference Librarian." *Wilson Library Bulletin* 21, no. (8): 603–4.

Rothstein, Samuel. 1955. *The Development of Reference Services through Academic Traditions: Public Library Practice and Special Librarianship.* ACRL Monograph Series, no. 14. Chicago: Association of College and Research Libraries.

Ryan, Sara. 1996. "Reference Service for the Internet Community: A Case Study of the Internet Public Library Reference Division." *Library and Information Science Research* 18, no. 3 (summer): 241–59.

Wyer, James I. 1930. *Reference Work: A Textbook for Students of Library Work and Librarians.* Chicago: American Library Association.

Chapter 3

Responding to Information Needs

In this chapter, we'll discuss

- the processes of information search and mediation;
- what reference librarians do better than anybody else;
- the roles of information resources, digital and print;
- crafting responses to reference inquiries;
- potential uses for reference-encounter transcripts; and
- collaborative opportunities and their potential importance.

The thrill of the hunt, the smell of the prey, digging out the fact or article or name or address or book that will answer the question and help somebody move on with their lives is, of course, what geeks and motivates most reference librarians. I've heard this from lots of librarians and students—we're the sort of people who loved researching papers in high school and college, sometimes even more than writing the papers themselves. It's the search that motivates us. That's not to say that the interview, the design and administration of services, the building of collections, aren't important aspects that many reference folks don't also enjoy, but in a sense this is what reference librarians do and why they got into the business in the first place. I think this is critically important and will return to it at the end.

So we've used our wiles to help the people we serve tell us what they need or want. We're used to in-person and telephone-based reference interviews, and now with e-mail and Web forms and other technological means we can solicit and refine these needs in new and potentially more fruitful and more widely accessible ways. The next step, obviously, is to try to find what users are looking for, or at least to do the best we can to find it or, sometimes, even discover that there's nothing to be found—which might even be the outcome they want (think patent searching).

In this chapter, I want to talk about this process of search and mediation, try to decompose the pieces of that process that are important, and think about them in our increasingly digital environment to see what, if anything, changes and then raise some issues about how to respond to users' needs in that environment. All of this, of course, takes place against the backdrop of what we've already discussed: the heritage, values, and motivations of reference; the technological and information world we face, our users, their communities, and their needs.

MEDIATION: WHAT WE DO BEST

We've already talked about the motivations behind the development of what we now know as reference services: there's a lot of information out there; it's hard to find; most people aren't really good at finding it or don't particularly care about the process of finding it; giving people help in finding what they need makes them feel better about libraries and engenders support; and they're better people for having received the help. But what do reference librarians really *do* that helps all that much? I'd like to propose several components of the reference process as things we do particularly well—perhaps, we might even claim, better than any other resource or profession—as a starting point for thinking about where we go from here. I'll put these all under the general heading of "mediation."

First of all, for many reference librarians, it's just what they do. It's tempting to say it's who they are. A lot of the students I've worked with over the years have "discovered" librarianship as a career, and particularly reference work, after careers elsewhere. They're often the sort of people whom friends and colleagues naturally turn to because they've always got the answers or know where to find them or have become the de facto organizers of information in their organizations. It's only after doing this for a few years that some of them stumble onto the fact that they could do just that part for a living—and get paid for it. Talking with such people after they make that discovery is a wondrous thing—it's almost as though they've been let out of prison or have had a marvelous epiphany. These people embody the *service orientation* of reference work: that reference professionals are there to provide the kind of direct service seen in question-answering, readers' advisory educational services and the like.

Contrast this with other information professionals, such as systems designers, database administrators, even technical-service librarians or catalogers, all of whom are absolutely vital to well-functioning information systems but whose orientation is often less directly focused on providing service to an eventual user than on constructing and maintaining the framework in which the information can be found. This is not, of course, to say that all or even most catalogers or acquisitions librarians or programmers don't appreciate and value the people who use their systems, but I would claim that their *primary* orientation is less toward service than among reference folks.

There is also evidence that this service orientation is also weaker among many of the ask-an-expert services that have appeared on the Web in the last couple of years (Janes and Hill, 2001). Our study showed that the number of follow-up or clarifying questions these services asked when responding to inquiries was pretty low, and many services asked none. (To be sure, this isn't the only measure of service orientation, but it's pretty important overall.) This was true of both the commercial services, often advertiser supported and looking to make a profit answering all comers, and the noncommercial services, run by individuals or organizations looking to educate and answer questions in their specific subject areas.

This segues nicely into *determining the need and understanding its context*; I've already talked quite a bit about this, so I won't belabor it here except to reemphasize its importance. We've all had the experience of doing a great job of answering the wrong question because we hadn't completely clarified it with the user. Is there anything more deflating than spending 15 minutes on a great search only to have the user say, "Gee, that's great, but I really wanted something different"? Sigh. I think most of us have also been on the wrong end of this, particularly with other kinds of services—such as information desks and voicemail-hell systems ("Press 6 to surrender now . . .")—with less skill in working with people to help them refine and structure their often ill-formed or overly broad inquiries. That's frustrating, too, and having the tools to support people as they resolve what kinds of information will most be of help to them is an important aspect of our work.

CONDUCTING THE SEARCH

Once we've got that clearer shared sense of what somebody wants or needs, then the search can begin. Searching isn't all that hard—how many millions of people type things into search-engine boxes on any given day?—but finding something worth the trouble is. Experienced and educated professionals are often among the most effective searchers, for a couple of reasons. They know the resources, databases, books, catalogs, indexes, how they are structured, what resources can be found using them, quirks of individual search interfaces and systems, and so on. They also know the tricks, the sophisticated search operators to allow searching with phrases or names or index terms; they can create complex Boolean searches; and they generally use their knowledge of which sources are most likely to yield good results for a given user's need.

The less obvious part of this is that they do all these things simultaneously and often without thinking about it. They are able to employ *multiple methods of searching* to attack any single information-search problem and in so doing construct more effective, complete, and thorough searches for those problems. So, for example, a few weeks ago at a public library reference desk a man asked me for books or magazines to help him build a go-cart. Thinking this was fairly straightforward and making sure we were on the same wavelength, I started searching. A keyword search on "go cart," "go-cart," "gocart," and a few other variants in the library catalog got me nowhere, which I found a bit puzzling, especially given the size of the library system's catalog. I decided to try looking for magazine articles, and similar searches in ProQuest and other general-interest periodical databases left me similarly bereft. I was starting to develop a healthy case of flop sweat with this poor man standing there, still with me, and although he seemed fine, I wasn't happy with myself. I started to think of other things I could try (*Ulrich's* to find a good magazine? General do-it-yourself books? Tell him it was the end of my shift?) and finally thought I'd give the Internet a crack. A search on "go cart magazine" in Google yielded a variety of interesting things, including what I was missing all along—in this world, they're called *go karts* (go figure), and the sport is called *karting,* which also happens to be the subject heading. Typed it into the catalog, and there it was. He was thrilled; I was relieved, and it was my ability to think of several ways of going about the search that saved me.

As a search is progressing, it's important to be able to *evaluate the resources* that are emerging from the search. While there are some standard criteria that are commonly useful, such as authority, currency, accuracy, accessibility, format, depth, and so on, this is almost always a your-mileage-may-vary sort of thing, and what would make sense for one user's need might well make less sense or even be completely wrong for another's. The key here, of course, is to evaluate the resources' value for a particular use, especially their appropriateness for that situation. Indeed, there are users for whom one or more of the standard criteria would even get in the way. Somebody looking for support for a particular point of view might find the "accuracy" of a resource to be a less important feature than that it agrees with what she or he believes. Sensitivity to this need for suitability—and being able to support it even when it might feel wrong—sets library services apart.

For as long as I've been teaching courses in online searching and reference, I've found that there are several questions that get asked quite regularly, especially by students who are new to the information-searching business. One of the questions that emerges early and often is "When do you stop searching?" My smart-aleck answer is usually "When you're done," and in this case it's even, in my opinion, the right answer. As experienced searchers know, there aren't any hard-and-fast rules about this, and there's surprisingly little about this in the reference or searching textbooks or literature. Sometimes, of course, there's nothing to be found, or at least not in the resources directly at hand, so the search is futile from the beginning, and the searcher may or may not have an instinct about that from the outset. And there are times when the search is intended to find that nothing exists.

But in general, I find that experienced folks have developed a sense of *when to stop the search*. It's probably a diminishing-returns phenomenon combined with a sense of what is likely to be out there and how much there will be. So the search begins and perhaps turns up an answer or a few good things, but there seems to be more, and the search continues; perhaps an initial sense that there won't be much is contradicted by finding quite a bit to begin, so that prolongs it, or conversely, a feeling that there will be a lot runs up against several brick walls. I've found that inquirers help here, too—I've had at least a couple of people physically back away from me when they've got as much as they want, even when I was continuing to find what I thought would be good things, perhaps even better than what I'd already found. I've restrained myself from chasing people as they make for the door, waving *The World Almanac* at them, but I've come close a time or two.

One of the intriguing aspects of digital reference is that the users are in many ways more removed from the process, and so they don't have the sense of how hard you're working, how much you're finding as the search proceeds, and how much longer it will take. In synchronous services that use chat, for example, keeping the user amused or busy while you're off doing something can be a challenge, and many of the call-center-based software packages permit you to take control of the users' browsers and do the search in front of them. (That must be quite an experience on the users' end.) In an asynchronous service, of course, it all goes on away from the users, which has its upsides and downsides. They're not there tapping their foot, waiting for us to stand and deliver on the spot, so we're not on the spot and can deliver a more complete, composed response, but by the same token some of the immediacy and the spontaneity and, certainly, the interactivity of the process is lost.

A large number of inquiries are of the simple question-and-answer type, or at least that's how both the users and we treat them. "What is the address of the Minnesota Historical Society?" "What's the derivation of the word *tragedy*?" "Where is the Princess Royal in the line of succession?" In most of these cases, the question is posed, searching goes on, an answer is found, it seems to be right, and the users are sent on their way. More detailed or involved information needs usually result in more detailed and involved processes, some feedback, a few blind alleys, some back and forth with the users. In many cases, though, we take the opportunity to weave in a little *education on the process and on the use of resources*. There are some places where this doesn't fly—when the CEO wants a report or an answer, he gets it, and this is not a chance to slyly instruct him on the use of the *D&B Million Dollar Directory*. But helping users to understand what they are and aren't likely to find on the Internet, why you prefer Google to Yahoo! for this sort of question, how to get the most out of search engines, how to evaluate Web sites based on domain name or authority, and so on, is often a natural part of the search-and-answer process, and the same is true in catalog searches, database searches, reference-book searches and the rest. We often think of academic and school librarians emphasizing this sort of thing, which is probably largely true, but public and even special librarians do it, too, and it's part of what we think makes our services different and better.

Finally, I'd add *tool making* to this list, which might initially come as a bit of a surprise. Most of the above is pretty standard stuff to your average reference librarian, but when you stop and think about it, as a profession, librarianship has been pretty darn good at tool making. Look at the organizational systems and structures we've developed over the decades to make some sort of order of the chaos that is the information world. (Yes, I know I said before that these universal systems are really hard for any individual to use, but that's inherent in the situation, and nobody else has come up with anything better than we have. Go play with Yahoo! for a few minutes *without using the search feature* if you need a reminder.)

Pathfinders, educational modules, courses, readers'-advisory guides, and now frequently-asked-question (FAQ) pages are all examples of devices that we've developed to help people even when we're not around. I'd include simple things we don't think twice about, like the vertical file and even signage, in this category. Perhaps most important and invisible is the amassing and management of collections of all stripes to provide more immediate access to high-quality resources to respond to the predicted needs of a community.

All of these are what distinguish reference services and librarians from other sources people turn to for information. This is often boiled down and referred to as *mediation* or, less clinically, *the human touch*. Not a bad way to think about it nor a bad professional approach, but now the question is how that human touch evolves in a more digitally mediated world.

DIGITAL REFERENCE PROCESS ISSUES

Now I'd like to discuss a number of issues raised by all of this; these are things that I've experienced in my own digital reference work, that have been talked about at conference sessions and on listservs or written about in the professional literature. This is by no means an exhaustive list; in fact, there are a great many other issues, but I want to talk about them separately, in the chapters on technology and building and institutionalizing a service. Here, though, I want to consider matters that are more immediate to the process itself.

Selecting the Right Resources

For example, what resources are or should be used in responding via some digital means? In a face-to-face encounter, the full panoply of resources are at your disposal, and whichever ones make the most sense or are most appropriate (or you know best, feel most comfortable with, are at hand) are the ones that are likely to be used. In telephone interactions, the range is similarly broad but restricted by what can be usefully conveyed on the phone; some libraries are able to fax, mail, or even courier documents, or leave something for the questioner to pick up.

In a digitally mediated world, it gets more complicated, and to a large extent it depends on the nature of the technology being used. We first consider digital resources, which fall into two main categories: free and not free. Free stuff on the Web is often worth exactly what you pay for it, but as we've all learned, there is also a great deal of good material on the Web, and we can no longer dismiss the Web as a valid resource for information work. However, it does bring with it all the difficulties about evaluation (authority, currency, accuracy, and so on), reinforcing the importance of that aspect of information work, as we discussed above. On the other hand, it's become very easy to search (though not necessarily easy to search well and with the precision we have been used to in such systems as catalogs and databases), and it's all—well—free. Libraries that have amassed collections of Web resources for their communities and audiences, including lists of ready-reference Web tools, built FAQs and pathfinders, and otherwise tried to make some sense of all of it have the right idea.

The not-free Web stuff is another story. Licensed versions of databases of newspaper and journal articles and article citations, as well as directories and other things we got used to in print and in dedicated online systems, have extended the reach and access to those materials and in some cases permitted better searching of them. (In some cases, of course, they've gone the other way. Am I the only one left who still goes back to Dialog for quick searches when I get frustrated with those dippy little boxes in journal databases that don't let me do what I want to do?)

They also require some sort of authentication, which is where it starts to get sticky. They're usually available to all (or some number of simultaneous number of) people in the library's community, but those people have to let the system know that, by entering a password or library-card number on a machine with a valid IP address or by using a machine in the building. But this raises the question of what *in the building* means, and I don't think the database vendors have yet come to terms with this question. If we view the "library" as the materials that have been collected and acquired for use by the community, then those folks who are surfing the library's Web site and databases at 1:00 in the morning are "in the library," right? But they're not "in the building." So if they don't have a library card or don't have it with them or are in Paraguay and can't get to an appropriate IP-addressable machine, they're out of luck. I think we need to help the vendors to understand that the walls of the building are less appropriate as measures of use of the library and to figure out better ways to allow the kind of access libraries are really paying for—often through the nose, I might add.

Choosing the Right Interfaces

A couple of other phenomena arise around these resources. There are a great many interfaces at work here, and they're all different. I can never keep straight which systems require me to use Boolean operators, and which are keyword based; it seems that every one has different truncation operators and rules about proximity and field search (if they allow them), and the "advanced" or "expert" interfaces are often confusing even for professionals, let alone laypeople. It's a mess and raises the question of educating people how to use them, especially since most users basically don't care. Not to harp on Dialog, but here's another example of its power and strength as a common interface to a wide variety of databases that allow high-quality and precise searching. Mind you, that interface is horrible and takes forever to learn, and its designers never came up with a decent end-user version, but the idea made sense 30 years ago and still does today. It's a shame it has largely passed away from the scene, and it makes me wonder whether something similar will have to arise again. This is another opportunity for the library community to use its purchasing muscle to encourage some standards and continuity among these variant systems to make things easier for everybody.

Recognizing the "Good Enough" Response

There's another, more pernicious problem here, and I've seen it especially while working with undergraduates at my university's reference desk. The full-text databases are great and of course are doing exactly what we've always wanted, providing direct access to the materials people want, not just lists of citations that often befuddle people anyway. However, the reaction I sometimes get when I tell people that the article they want, which I believe would be perfect for their paper or project, isn't available in full text but is in a bound journal just upstairs on the third floor is not encouraging. Have you seen it? A heavy sigh, eyes turned upward and a general sagging of the shoulders. Translation: well, I don't want it that badly. Can we try Google? What else have you got that I don't have to go upstairs for?

Now, of course, they're right. Users often want a response that is good enough—not perfect but optimal—and they're only willing to invest a certain amount of effort to get it. It is certainly the case that a sizable number of patrons do indeed happily go up and make the copies, but just between us, I love being able to print stuff from my computer at the office or at home and have even been guilty of just using what's easily available from time to time. This is a variant of the "if it's not in the online database it doesn't exist" phenomenon, which we've known about for decades, and it's unlikely to go away. We just need to be able to help those people who can hear it understand that there's really good stuff upstairs, or wherever it is, and it's probably worth their while to go and explore it.

Utilizing Print Resources

Which leads us to print. Print resources are, of course, a substantial component of most libraries' collections and likely contain a large majority of the useful information in any given collection. But analog media (and here I'd include anything in print, analog images, sound or moving-image recordings, microforms, realia, and so on) can't be sent across a digital line. Text can be typed in, documents of all kinds can be scanned or digitized, but this is often laborious or expensive and may take too long.

And there's an argument to be made that if people are asking questions digitally, via e-mail, chat, or whatever, they should get their answers *in the same way they asked the question*, or at least a digital answer should be strongly preferred, since that's how the users approached the service. I think that argument has a lot going for it and largely subscribe to it, but I would never respond with a digital resource I didn't think was appropriate just because the question came in via e-mail; however, if there's a "good" answer available digitally, I'd probably use it over a "better" print response.

Respecting Intellectual Property and Copyright

These questions of licensing and of digitizing analog resources for digital distribution raise a set of intellectual-property and copyright issues here, which nobody wants to touch because they're really hard. My understanding is that most licensing agreements don't take into account copying and pasting into an e-mail or Web response to library patrons, let alone nonpatrons from outside the service community. Typing in a fact or a paragraph from a book may well be fair use, but how much can you scan or digitize? In the post–Digital Millennium Copyright Act world, these are legitimate and looming questions. I'm pleased to say that the American Library Association is doing great work in educating the library community about these issues and advocating our perspectives on them in legislative, executive. and even judicial realms.[1]

GUIDELINES AND POLICIES FOR ASYNCHRONOUS REFERENCE SERVICES

This discussion of what kinds of resources you can use and how you might be able to send resources to users leads directly to the idea of *guidelines for response.* I'm sure a number of libraries have assembled sets of guidelines or even policies for responding to reference inquiries in general, as well as via digital means. In this discussion, I'm drawing mainly from ones I know well: the Internet Public Library's policy on answering reference questions, the Virtual Reference Desk's "Facets of Quality for Digital Reference Services" www.vrd.org/facets–10–00.shtml), QuestionPoint's "Member Guidelines" www.questionpoint.org/web/members/memberguidelines.html), and RUSA's "Guidelines for Behavioral Performance of Reference and Information Services Professionals" www.ala.org/rusa/stnd_behavior.html), which although not specific to digital reference, is nonetheless of interest. I'll focus on the IPL's document, though, because I was involved in its development, it's specific to digital reference-question answering, and it encompasses much, but not all, of what is found in the others. I also really like it. I'll quote directly from the document and discuss each of the four sections in turn.

Guideline 1: What to Do before Trying to Answer a Question

The first section talks about things to do before trying to answer a question:

- Read the entire question and the item's history in QRC (claims, follow-ups, etc.).
- Try to anticipate the age and the English language comprehension level of the patron you are writing for. Don't censor on the basis of this guess, but do be aware of potential difficulties.
- Anticipate the kind of answer wanted. To some extent this will be indicated by which category the question is in: sources

or factual. Don't become so caught up in answering the question that you forget what the patron really wants.

- If necessary, clarify the patron's question. If you can think of at least two ways to answer the question, consider writing to the patron. If you can't think of any way to answer the question, definitely write to the patron.
- Take note of the "needed by" date. Don't let it pass once you've claimed a question. If you will miss the "needed by" date, write to the patron in advance with a warning and explanation.

QRC, I should explain, is the homegrown software package the IPL's been using since 1995 to manage its digital reference operation. It was developed specifically for this purpose, so it can be used to efficiently receive and accept questions, administer the process of answering, communicate with patrons and other librarians, and send answers out. It also archives all communications of the IPL, including reference questions received and answered.

The first bullet above refers to "the item's history in QRC"; this tells anyone looking whether anyone else has worked on the question and posted potential answers, clues, ideas, things they've tried or looked at, and so on, to give an idea of where it stands and prevent duplication of effort. The second and third bullets look much like familiar reference practice: what does the patron want, how much, at what level, in what language (many of IPL's questions are international and come from people who may have little facility with English, but similar conditions would obtain elsewhere as well)? The fourth speaks to the nature of the reference interview in this domain; services such as IPL that use extensive forms rely on those forms to get the bulk of the information from the patron to save time. When that doesn't work, writing back with clarifying questions—even though people don't respond about one third of the time—is about the only way to move forward responsibly without guessing what the person really wants. Finally, the form asks for a deadline, after which the answer isn't needed; respecting the deadline (even though it is often months or years in the future or may even be "don't care") is important.

A digression on these need-by dates. The IPL has always thought that it gets a substantial number of questions that are just things on people's minds as they run across the site. Many other questions are more immediate needs that people have sought help for, but it's common to see these extended deadlines or no date at all. Here is where I think digital reference—specifically e-mail based—shines. It provides for the sorts of questions that people really would like an answer to but for which they're willing to wait to get a good answer and allow the librarian to compose that complete and high-quality answer. I love those questions: "What's the name of this poem my grandmother used to recite to me?"— that sort of thing. They're fun, and people are often really grateful for the help. A real opportunity for us, I think.

Guideline 2: When to Give Up

Here are a couple of points on researching and when to give up:

- If possible, answer questions using reliable Internet resources, giving preference to the works in the IPL Ready Reference Collection. Do not, however, use the Internet to the exclusion of print resources. If you aren't sure what print resources are available to aid your search, don't forget to ask other reference librarians.
- Ideally, it should take no more than an hour to answer an IPL reference question. Obviously, not all questions are that simple; but taking into account the resources and mission of the IPL, you should stop to evaluate your progress after about 45 minutes of searching. If you haven't found anything useful by then, seriously consider unclaiming the question or setting it to NEED_HELP. This is not a hard-and-fast rule, and your own experience will help you set your own limits.

The first point here is a variation on my earlier comment about answering people in the way they asked. In IPL's case, of course, the collection consists solely of freely available Web resources, so it is natural that that would be where the focus lies; other libraries would certainly decide to emphasize their strengths. The stopping problem arises here, too, but again, the IPL is unique because of its educational focus: it is a way for people to learn how to be better reference librarians in a digital world. Forty-five minutes to an hour may well be appropriate in some circumstances, in others less, perhaps more in a few places, but I think it is reasonable to assume that almost any digital reference encounter will take longer to complete, from the librarian's perspective, than it previously has.

Why is that? Largely because in most of the digital scenarios currently under discussion or experimentation, typing is involved, and for most people, typing takes longer than speaking. Even very fast typists will find that much of the chatting and discussion and explanation that we're used to doing verbally, not to mention the potential back-and-forth of an interview, takes substantially longer when using e-mail or chat than it does in person or over the phone. It's a simple fact and is something that would need to be factored into decisions about developing, implementing, staffing, and evaluating any such services. There's less immediate pressure on this typing aspect (and thus less impact on the patron and the librarian) in an e-mail environment than in chat, but it's there nonetheless. This is also true for any digitization of analog documents, not to mention cutting and pasting of URLs, e-mail addresses, and so on. In a chat or call-center environment, which enables the librarian to send a page address or direct a patron's browser to go directly to a page ("pushing" the page), this is mitigated somewhat. You still have the difficulty of keeping patrons amused while you're looking for something to push to them, but they are at least getting it right away instead of having to wait hours or days (or more) for a response.

Guideline 3: Mandatory Response Components

Here's the third section I want to discuss, on mandatory components to responses:

Salutation: Open with a greeting of some kind, with or without the patron's name.

If we don't know the patron's name, "Dear IPL Patron" or "Greetings from the IPL" works well. If we have their names, choosing between addressing them by first or last name can be a matter of personal style. Try to base your decision on the question we received. If the question was couched as a professional or business letter, respond in kind. If the style was less formal, then you may address the patron by first name if you are comfortable doing so.

Acknowledgment of Question: Say that you are writing to answer the question.

This may take the form of a "thank you for your question about woodchucks" or "I'm writing to answer your question about bugs."

Common sense, really, but a nice touch. This is partially trying to make up for the lack of personal connection with users in this environment and partially trying to make it as pleasant a process for both librarian and patron. Perhaps this is the e-mail equivalent of smiling, appearing approachable, seeming interested, and so on, which we find in the RUSA guidelines.

In a chat or instant-messaging environment, there are other mores in play, and those should be followed. There's an interesting balance to be struck here; experienced chat and instant-messaging users have lots of abbreviations and signs to take the place of words and phrases, to save typing (*lol* for "laughing out loud," for example, and the emoticons we've become used to in e-mail). Even more elaborate—and cryptic for the uninitiated—abbreviations are evolving among people who communicate with instant-messaging services via cell phones; they're trying to save screen space as well. This is called SMS, for "short message service," and it can get pretty intense:

WERV U BIN? PPL R starting to use SMS abbreviations all

the time, OTOH not everyone understands what BCNU means. 2 SIT W/ SOM1 by MOB or email, SMS abbreviations R GR8. :-)

Where have you been? People are starting to use SMS abbreviations all the time, on the other hand not everyone understands what 'be seeing you' means. To stay in touch with someone by mobile or email SMS abbreviations are great.[2]

As we develop services in those environments as well, we'll have to figure out the appropriate mixture of those kinds of abbreviations and the professional tone I think most of us would expect in a reference-type encounter. Whether anybody else thinks that's important or not may well be another matter.

Answer: Answer the question the patron asks.

If you veer off from the actual question, be sure to explain your departure. If they ask for a factual answer and you can only provide sources, say so and explain why. If any part of your answer could be construed as medical or legal advice, insert a disclaimer that you are not a physician/lawyer, that you are only reporting what you found and that the patron should consult an appropriate authority before acting on the information provided.

Cite your source: Always tell the patron where your information comes from.

- If at any point you insert your own opinion, be sure that it is clearly marked as such.
- When citing Web sources, be sure to include the address on a separate line, starting with the "http://"—that will make it easier for the patron to cut and paste the address and have it work in any browser. Be sure not to include any punctuation after the URL, as this may interfere with its function. It will also make it easier for URLs to be identified quickly in an answer, by both humans and machines.

- Exception: if the URL is the icky-looking result of a search interface, give the URL for the search page and then give the exact search string you used. If applicable, don't forget to mention in these cases that you are only providing a sample of the results and that the patron may want to look at more.

Again, mainly common sense and experience with a variety of e-mail systems, browsers, word processors, and so on. The last point in particular is important not only for the mechanical and logistic aspects of dealing with increasingly lengthy URLs that have imbedded searches and other unrepeatable character strings. It's important also because of the lack of immediate feedback from and interaction with the questioner. I often find that when I do a search and get several potential responses, it's easier to tell the patrons how I searched and characterize the results quite generally and then encourage them to repeat the search and evaluate the responses on their own. If my results yield something truly awful, untrustworthy, contradictory, and so on, I'll mention that; but rather than impose my judgment on a largish potential set of resources, I'll let the patrons do it. Of course, if I find one or two good things, I'll just send those along, but I might also indicate there was more to be found and suggest further searching if the patrons see fit.

> *Show how you got there*: Let the patron know how you found the answer.

- If it came off the Web, tell how you found it (e.g., what search engine, using what search string). When citing a search engine, mention that it's a search engine. If you just say "Magellan," they may have no clue. Also be sure to include the URL for the search engine.
- Try to avoid subscription-based Web services like Encyclopædia Britannica and the New York Times.
- Exceptions:
  - if you went through the Yahoo! hierarchy, or something similar that shows the path in the URL, just say so.

- If you started with a search engine but then just started clicking links tell them that; don't include every step you made, even if you remember.
- If you use a source that you know off the top of your head (Amazon, POTUS, Internet Movie Database, etc.) say that and give the URL and a brief explanation. ("Amazon is a huge online bookstore with a search engine that's like Books In Print online, only bigger.")
- If your answer came out of a print source that isn't a standard reference book (dictionary, almanac, encyclopedia), try to give a Library of Congress Subject Heading (LCSH) so the patron can find similar if not identical books in a traditional library. Give a brief explanation of LCSH mentioning that most U.S. libraries will use those entries in their subject catalogs.

Guideline 4: Transcript Records

Here you see the instructional and educational mission emerging; I think this aspect of digital reference is particularly important because it leaves a trace. I know that when I'm interacting with people on the desk, a good deal of what I'm saying about the sources I'm using, how I got there, how else one might approach a similar problem, is just drifting away into the ether. It's not that the patrons are thick; it's just not a language they're used to hearing; and remember: they don't care. So I try to print pages that include URLs, search strings, and so on, to help them remember what we did. But here the entire "conversation," if you will, is recorded—both their question (often the librarians at the IPL just quote the users' questions right back at them, which is easy to do) and the response, complete with all these aspects. Then it's available to them for as long as they keep the response, and they can consult it and perhaps use ideas or techniques in subsequent searching. Or not. But at least they've got it, and the librarian has taken advantage of a teachable moment, even when never confronting the users asynchronously. Similar things could be said about transcripts that are the result of chat, instant-messaging, or call-center-software interactions.

Those transcripts are an interesting development as well. With a very few exceptions, reference work over the decades has left no trace: it's been an ephemeral, transaction-based enterprise, mostly based on conversation, gesture, and other interpersonal interactions. Now, though, with most technological systems, it is possible to capture the entire transaction: the initial question, the clarification of the need, the response, and in some cases even the search process. This has several fascinating ramifications. As I've said, as an artifact for the user it can be valuable as an enduring record for future exploration. It also can be a useful tool for evaluating staff, services, resources, collections and their use, and so on.

It also can scare the whim-whams out of people, especially librarians who are used to ephemeral reference. Reference can now be different work, because other people can be watching. There are obvious privacy concerns at work, particularly for users, but this concern can run deeper. There may well be reference librarians who prefer a transient interaction, because then there's no way somebody else can later come back and question their professional judgments, searching ability, interviewing skills, even typing ability. Of course this concern could exist and is somewhat understandable, but let's face it—our colleagues who compile indexes and cataloging records and other artifacts have been dealing with those concerns for decades, and they seem to be getting along just fine. Being worried that somebody might look over your shoulder smacks of professional insecurity and perhaps even a fear or arrogance—nobody could or should be able to tell you or help you to do your job more effectively. Anybody worried about that sort of scrutiny probably shouldn't be a reference librarian.

Guideline 5: User Privacy Policies

I want to return to the privacy concern on the part of the user—this is a legitimate worry and must be dealt with. Most jurisdictions have laws protecting the privacy of circulation records; it's unlikely they would also cover reference transactions, but I'd just as soon avoid litigation on this. When constructing a digital reference service, librarians should be sure to post a clear, understandable, and legally viable privacy policy so people know what kinds of personal information will be collected and what, if anything, will be done with that information. At a minimum, people should be reassured that their names and e-mail addresses and other personal information will never be resold or reused without their knowledge and permission and that certainly no information will be revealed that would identify them in conjunction with their request. In this way, digital reference can actually be more protective of privacy than in-person reference, which usually requires people to reveal their potentially embarrassing or private or personal information needs *in public* and *in a loud, clear voice*. It staggers the imagination to conceive of the number of reference questions that *haven't* been asked because of that situation; perhaps allowing such people to ask anonymously and privately will be a boon for them.

The privacy concern also arises because of the ability to archive these transcripts. This is a great idea, and a powerful one. Think of what might be achieved by gathering these professionally crafted answers with high-quality results of thoughtful searches to questions of all stripes from all kinds of people. Making such collections of asked and answered questions searchable, by professionals and—perhaps with personal information suitably excised—users, could put Ask Jeeves and similar systems to shame.

Except I don't think it will happen, or at least not in a panacea-type way. My experience is that (a) relatively few questions are direct repeats, and thus these archives don't come into play that often; (b) removing personal information is often very difficult because people imbed it in their messages, even on a form where it's not hard to strip out fields with names, e-mail addresses, phone numbers, and the like; and (c) it's pretty difficult to search such archives. We do know a bit about searching for documents by taking advantage of our knowledge about what's likely to be there and how it's structured, but searching here is very different. These archives aren't documents; they're files of questions and answers, and the language that's used to pose the questions and frame the responses can be very colloquial, vague, and therefore tricky to search. I don't mean to imply here that it's a bad idea to build archives of questions and add search capability; at the very least, they can be useful for evaluating a service, finding out more about users and what their needs are, and helping with collection development as well as refining reference service and Web-site design, but I wouldn't rely on searching these archives in any substantial way for large numbers of future questions. I could be completely wrong on this one, but so far I'm unconvinced.

Guideline 6: Closure

Closing: Sign your name, with at least some kind of closing (thanks, I hope this helps, feel free to write back, etc.).

Another attempt to personalize and humanize the process as much as possible. The QRC software has another nice feature—it automatically appends a signature file to all outgoing messages, so the librarians don't have to add their own, and it nicely rounds out the message. Here's mine (the nifty ASCII art on the left is a replica of the IPL logo):

```
[/I\]   Joseph Janes
I-+-I   iplref@ipl.org—http://www.ipl.org/ref/
[\I/]   "the Day Begins at Midnight"
```

Using software such as QRC also avoids the question of whether to give patrons a librarian's individual e-mail address; people certainly have the option, but QRC provides a central point for all communication back and forth. In other libraries, librarians may well want to give out their personal e-mail address, to attempt to build a connection with their users, encourage them to use their services, and so on. Others may prefer a central e-mail address or use of other means (chat, and so on) to save their personal in boxes from reference mail.

This kind of closing is also an opportunity to make sure that you've answered the question that's been asked and in the way that was wanted. I usually say something like "I hope this completely answers your question; if not, let us know, and we'll try again. Thanks for using the IPL," which at least opens the door for people to respond if there's something missing, I've misunderstood, gotten it completely wrong, or whatever. In practice, I've almost never had that happen, and I don't think many others have either, but that doesn't mean this isn't a good idea.

Asynchronous Guideline Checklist

Finally, here are the IPL guidelines on things to be sure to do:

- Proofread your answers for grammar, style, and spelling.
- Check to make sure your links work.
- Make sure your source has some basis (or, at the very least, appearance) of authority.
- Avoid using library/Internet jargon without at least explaining it. Examples of this include: ILL (or even Interlibrary Loan, unless you explain what it is), OPAC, LCSH, URL. It is also better to refer to academic libraries as "college" or "university" libraries.
- Be sure to answer or address all parts of a question, and don't stop short just because you find incomplete information in one source. For example, if a patron asks for the date of a particular event, and all you find in one source is the year or month of the event, look harder to find the actual date. This even applies when one source says that no one knows anything more specific. If you repeatedly find that same assertion then pass it along to the patron, but don't trust the first source that tells you so.

Sort of a checklist of important things to keep in mind, none of which is likely surprising or groundbreaking. A number of these points were developed to help students who were learning to become librarians in the first place, who may have had little or no experience in reference before coming to the IPL; some are for professionals who volunteer for the IPL service to learn more about digital reference work as they mount their own services. As such, these guidelines are an intriguing mix of fairly straightforward reference practice and some things unique to the Internet environment. Exactly the same and completely different.

REAL-LIFE QUESTIONS AND RESPONSES

Patricia Memmott, the head of reference for the IPL, has graciously consented to letting me share some of her work. Here are several examples of actual questions and responses from IPL, demonstrating not only how these guidelines work in practice but also great reference technique (names and e-mail addresses of questioners have been removed):

Idiom Search

Needed by: 1/7/02

Question:
I need to know what the idiom means and where it originated? The idiom is "pull the rug out from under you"

location: Fort Wayne, IN
grade: 8th
school: Yes

Hello from the IPL,

Thanks for your question about the meaning and origin of the idiom "pull the rug out from under you."

I found an entry for this idiom in the Cambridge International Dictionary of Idioms at:
http://dictionary.cambridge.org/define.asp?key=rug*1+0

It provides this definition: "to suddenly take away help or support from someone, or to suddenly do something which causes many problems for them"

It does not provide any information on the idiom's origin, however. I found this dictionary by looking in the IPL's English Dictionaries section at:

http://www.ipl.org/ref/RR/static/ref28.05.00.html

To further research its origins, you may want to try looking through the sources recommended in the IPL's Word and Phrase Origins Pathfinder at:
http://www.ipl.org/ref/QUE/PF/etymology.html

Good luck with your research, and thanks for asking the IPL.

A simple response giving a direct response to the question, citing the source and how it was found, reinforcing the use of the IPL collection, and suggesting a pathfinder for future reference.

Franklin's Passed Gas

Here the response is to a fellow librarian, so the language is a bit different, but it walks through the process, including a nice piece of searching and asking if the answer is what was wanted (albeit in this case one step removed, of course).

Question:
I am trying to track down an essay, written by Ben Franklin on the benefits of passing gas for a patron at the library I work at. I can only find confirmation that he actually did write an essay on that and he sent it to the Royal Academy at Brussels for publication. Any help you could give me would be appreciated!!! Thanks!

location: Mauston, WI, US
area: Literature

reason: A patron would like a copy of it.
answer_type: factual
sources_consulted: Brief search on the Internet. Found out
that he did write the essay on this page.
http://teched.vt.edu/gcc/HTML/PrintingsPast/EccentricBen.html

Greetings from the Internet Public Library,

Thanks for your question about locating Ben Franklin's essay on the benefits of passing gas. I believe I have located
the piece in question, which is actually titled "A Letter to a
Royal Academy," and is available online on this "Writings
of Benjamin Franklin" site:
http://members.tripod.com/~benfranklin4/bf7/royalacad.html

I first discovered this by doing an Advanced search on the
Altavista search engine
http://www.altavista.com/
for the terms:
"benjamin franklin" NEAR fart
which led to an Amazon page for a collection of Franklin's
works, titled "Fart Proudly." By doing more searches on this
title, I found this "Founding Father Flatulence" page:
http://classic.sacbee.com/smile/required/required_061997/
required.html

which provided the correct title of (and an excerpt from) the
letter in question, which I used to find the page with the full
text.

Let us know if this isn't what your patron was looking for,
and thanks for consulting the IPL!

History Videos for Kids

Question:
Am looking for videos adapted for young viewers on subjects
included on history curriculum of my fifth grade daughter—

American history from the colonists to the civil rights movement. Please let me know what you recommend and where
to find them.

location: Gloucester, VA, USA
area: History
reason: I want this information to help bring her social studies class alive. She loves the History channel but does not like
social studies class.
answer_type: sources
sources_consulted: Looked at Reference Section of the VA
SOLs.

Greetings from the IPL,

Thanks for your question about finding educational videos
on U.S. history for a 5th grader. This was quite tricky, as
many sites that sell educational videos don't make it possible
to narrow a search both by grade level and by subject area. I
was finally successful in finding one, the "Social Studies
School Service" at:
http://socialstudies.com/

If you go to their search screen at:
http://socialstudies.com/c/@1kkrJgwaYILKQ/Pages/
search.html
and select "Videocassettes" from the Media menu, "Grades
4–9" from the Grade Level menu, and "U.S. History" from
the Subjects menu, and then click on "Search," you will be
able to retrieve descriptions of 156 titles that meet these criteria. A few even have "video previews" that let you watch
the first five minutes over the Internet.

I found this site by doing a Google search
http://www.google.com/
for the terms: "social studies" "lesson plans" videos "grade
level"

Two of the lesson plan sites that came up in the results listing both mentioned the above site as the best place to find videos.

It's also worth noting that this while this site might be one of the best for actually identifying titles that might interest you, it may not be the cheapest place to buy them. Alternately, as these are educational videos, you might be able to obtain them from your local public library. Many libraries, if they don't own a particular video, offer the option of using an "Interlibrary Loan" to help patrons borrow from another library that does have the video.

Let us know if these suggestions aren't helpful to you, and thanks for asking the IPL!

I like this response for several reasons. Beyond what I've mentioned above, I think Patricia's hit the right tone, helping the person to understand the environment she's in, encouraging her to be critical in her evaluation of these sites, making sure she knows where Google is (not everybody does; it only seems that way), explaining some of the details of the search process but not too many, and of course, stressing the importance of the local library.

GUIDELINES FOR SYNCHRONOUS REFERENCE

The IPL guidelines really apply only to the asynchronous e-mail world, since that's all the IPL does. They're based largely on experience in both the traditional and the digital reference worlds. Similar guidelines for synchronous, or chat-based, services are only now just arising.

This interesting list comes from LSSI, one of the major vendors of digital reference software, and has been produced to aid in judging an award for outstanding chat reference work.[3]

While some of these are obviously specific to the award process (item 1, for example), we see many similarities with the IPL list and several things that are new: concern for the nature of the interview (questions 4–6 as well as 8); time, from the user's perspective (questions 2 and 10); accuracy (11); and evaluation (12).

Guidelines for the Samuel Swett Green Exemplary Virtual Reference Award:

A Checklist for Model Reference Transactions:

The LSSI Transcript Evaluation Form

Prepared by Dr. John V. Richardson Jr., LSSI Presidential Scholar
Copyright © 2002 by Library Systems and Services, LLC

The following questions will be weighted differently (e.g., questions 11 & 12 would have greater weight than others).

1. Have you removed librarian and user identifying information?
2. How long was the user waiting?
3. Was the librarian dealing with more than one inquirer?
4. Are open-ended questions used at the outset of the transaction to clarify the information need?
5. Has the librarian confirmed what other resources the user has already checked?
6. Is there a closed-ended question at the end of the initial interview confirming that the librarian understands the user's inquiry?
7. Did the librarian tell the user what s/he is doing as the transaction progresses?
8. Did the librarian use some variation of this closed-ended question "Did this answer your question" at the end of the transaction?
9. Is there an overall impression of:
   a) "a courteous disposition,

    b) sympathy,
    c) cheerfulness,
    d) patience, and
    e) enthusiasm in working with inquirers?"
10. Is the session duration appropriate to the query (or too long or too short)?
11. Is the question answered correctly?
    a) if the question is not fully answered, is the user referred to an appropriate resource?
    b) if the question is answered, is the user given a specific, authoritative source(s) to support the librarian's answer?
12. Is there evidence of the user's satisfaction?

Transcript Excerpt from Synchronous Reference

I'd love to reprint the transcript of the first session given this award, but it's miles long, representing a session of over 50 minutes. Instead, I thought I'd include a briefer transcript, taken from the report of a poster session presented at ALA by Matt Marsteller and Paul Neuhaus, at Carnegie Mellon University, of their experiences using LivePerson.

> **Andy:** Hello Dizzy, how may I help you today?
> **Dizzy:** I was wondering if you had any idea where i could information on incan foods . . . namely how to make them.
> **Dizzy:** find information . . . sorry
> **Andy:** Where have you looked so far?
> **Dizzy:** mainly on the internet, for about the last three days and i havent turned up much . . . nothing actually
> **Andy:** Can you hold for a couple of minutes and I will check some things?
> **Dizzy:** yes i can
> **Andy:** Thank you for waiting. I'll be with you momentarily.
> **Dizzy:** thanks
> **Andy:** You may get the information you need from an encyclopedia. I will push you a page for online encyclopedias.
> **Dizzy:** ok thank you

> Andy: http://www.library.cmu.edu/Research/Genref/ency.html
> Andy: I tried the Encyclopedia and saw a couple items listed under canning and also "vacuum packaging."
> Dizzy: ok . . . thank you
> Andy: I tried the Encyclopaedia Britannica.
> Dizzy: ok . . . thank you . . . that was all i needed.
> Andy: If this does not have the information you need let me know and I can check elsewhere.
> Dizzy: ok . . .
> Andy: Thank you for waiting. I'll be with you momentarily.
> Andy: Unexpectedly left call
> Staller: Call terminated unexpectedly
> Andy: Party left call[4]

This is pretty quick stuff; they don't indicate in the report how long this took, but I'll bet it wasn't too long. Notice how the librarian (Andy) is trying really hard to do the whole reference thing, but quickly, and how as soon as the inquirer gets what he (?) thinks he wants, he's gone. Fascinating.

PROFESSIONAL COLLABORATIONS FOR PROVIDING REFERENCE SERVICES

Beyond providing the response to any given need, these technologies now open the door to collaboration in much more meaningful and extensive ways than has so far been possible. The opportunity to work with librarians at other institutions is tantalizing because it's something that has been tried with varying degrees of success over the years; services have existed for quite some time that allowed libraries to send questions of great difficulty or beyond the scope of their collections to a central place for expert support and greater resources. It would be easy to replicate those sorts of services in a digital domain, but an even more powerful idea arose very quickly and even predated widespread use of the Internet.

Stumpers-L

Stumpers-L, the listserv for difficult reference questions, has been around for years and still thrives, taking advantage of what the Internet is best at: connecting people and drawing on their collective strengths. It's blindingly simple: you ask a question, hundreds of people see it, somebody knows the answer or can find it, and the answer comes back to you. It works; it's simple, usually fairly quick; and there's a critical mass of people who use it.

The next obvious question is why Stumpers or something a whole lot like it hasn't become even more popular. I subscribe, and over the last several days there have been a few new questions posted and answers received, but nothing like the hundreds and thousands of difficult, partially answered (or not answered at all or, worse yet, unknowingly incorrectly answered) questions we know are out there. I've pondered this question for a while and have to admit I don't know the answer, and I suspect there are several possibilities, all potentially true to some degree. Perhaps Stumpers is too slow in getting an answer for an immediate information need. Perhaps the responses that come back are incomplete, incorrect, inaccurate, off the mark, and so on. From my experience, these don't seem to be the case, although the only quality-control mechanism is other librarians' seeing the responses come through—and that's not a bad mechanism at all. Perhaps not enough people know about it, or people have grown fatigued with reading it over time. Perhaps it's something else.

Do Reference Collaborations Go Against the Grain?

Or perhaps it's something about the way reference librarians have been trained and are used to doing their job. My gut instinct, and I cannot provide much evidence to this effect, is that most reference librarians see themselves as highly skilled but independent professionals, and when somebody comes up to them with an information need, by God, they're going to get an answer. There is very little in the professional or educational literature about collaboration in the reference world, and I wouldn't be surprised if many reference folks think of sending their questions off to be answered by somebody else as a sign of weakness or professional failure and would therefore be more than a little hesitant to do it. To be sure, librarians working at reference desks often ask for help from a colleague standing right there or offer an idea if they overhear a question they think they can assist with, but that's a much more personal situation, and the people involved know each other and trust each other. Cooperative or tiered services have been around for quite some time and have been moderately successful in their own way, but there may be something about wide-scale cooperative services that goes against the grain of the way reference is, and has been, done. This would seem to diminish the potential importance of such large-scale services, and indeed, in the early stages of the Library of Congress's cooperative service, there was some difficulty in encouraging members to *submit* questions, with no lack of people to *answer* them.

Are those services doomed, then, to play relatively minor roles in reference work in the future? I certainly hope not, because they have the potential to revolutionize the way we think about personal service. If QuestionPoint or something like it were to take off and be a major success, we'd've reached the reference equivalent of the promised land. Think about it—patrons somewhere, anywhere, have an information need they're itching to deal with. They approach their local library and ask that question. In this scenario, let's assume nothing about the kinds of patrons, community, library, or need or how they present the need. Let's just say the need is presented and their library can't quite come up with the goods; either the collection is too limited, it's closed, it doesn't have the staff or expertise or technology that would be needed— whatever. It's not able to do what needs to be done, so the library passes the question off. The question goes to a richly connected web of librarians of all kinds and shapes and sizes, and via some mechanism (automatic matching by subject area, type of library, geography, language, and so on, or by selection by somebody who thinks he or she can handle it or by some other reasonable way), it goes to a librarian who can give a good, complete, appropriate response. That librarian assembles that response, and it goes directly back to the users with a notation that their library participates in this web to provide the highest-quality service to the community.

There are lots of issues here—governing boards that wonder why their library is answering questions for people all over the countryside, technological compatibility, licensing agreements and intellectual-property concerns, timing, staffing, the balance between a local and a global service, paying for the overhead involved, marketing and publicity, load balancing, and so on and so on—but the basic idea gives us the power we've always wanted. Recall our definition of *reference* in Chapter 1: *the provision of direct, professional assistance to people who are seeking information, at the time and point of need.* This would seem to fit the bill nicely. And yet to make it work, we not only need the richly connected web of librarians, but we also need those librarians to cough up the tough questions so the web has something to do. This will require some real effort on the part of some people and some trust building on the part of any collaborative service. To get beyond the isn't-this-a-great-idea stage and become a valuable production-level entity, it'd have to come across sufficiently well to make both inquirers and forwarding librarians happy enough to come back. Technical, legal, and administrative challenges are easy; getting people to play in the sandbox is the tough part. And notice, by the way, that the lack of assumption about library type, method of asking the question, and so on, didn't make much difference, and it shouldn't, *from the inquirers' point of view.* It's their job to pose questions, and it's ours to get them responded to. We should make the hoops that get a question into any reference service as few and far between as possible and impose the burden of massaging it into something useful on professionals who know what they're doing.

Ask-an-Expert Services

While we're on the subject of cooperation, there is another potential source of assistance and another group of people who might be of great value in helping to respond to difficult or detailed needs. Over the last several years, hundreds of Web-based ask-an-expert services have arisen, and many of them provide good answers to questions. I'm particularly fond of subject-specialized services because they tend to be more focused and proceed from a mission to share their knowledge about their areas with a wider world. As you might expect, there's a wide variety of these services, from the very sophisticated ones, often maintained by professional organizations, to individual people with Web pages, who may or may not actually know what they're talking about. Without a doubt, the very best source from which to help find high-quality ask-an-expert services is the Virtual Reference Desk project at Syracuse University (www.vrd.org); it provides assistance to individuals and groups wanting to start or improve services, recognizes exemplary ones, sets standards for quality services, and maintains lists of services that meet those standards, as well as maintaining DIG_REF, the premier listserv, and running the best conference in the world on digital reference matters. I have nothing but the highest praise for VRD and its staff and recommend without hesitation its work to anyone interested in high-quality information service.

The use of ask-an-expert services can rankle some people—they're not librarians, after all—and there are legitimate questions about them. In selecting one, it would be wise to evaluate its point of view (stated or unstated and sometimes, of course, the best response to a question might well be one that emerges from a specific perspective or even bias), policies about kinds of questions it'll answer, statements about time for an answer to be received, approach and philosophy, and so on. Services that support themselves by advertising or charging for answers are not inherently less good than ones that don't, but care should be taken to be sure that commercialism doesn't get in the way of providing a good, useful, accurate, and appropriate response.

Answering In-House Questions Digitally

Finally, there's an intriguing phenomenon that has arisen in the last couple of years around digital reference services: questions from within the library when the library is open, sometimes even from computers within sight of the reference desk. I recall with some amusement a posting to DIG_REF a couple of years ago from an academic librarian describing this phenomenon with great righteousness and high dudgeon. "Why don't these people just get off their butts and ask a question at the desk like they're supposed to? Don't they understand that that's what we're here for? They can't be serious about their questions if they can't be bothered to get up and ask us." Blah blah, rant rant rant.

I forbore responding and telling this poor guy that his questions were self-answering. I probably wouldn't approach him if I were a student in his library either, because I'd guess that his attitude toward his students exuded from his every pore like a pheromone, driving them off like a repellant, but his posting was fun to read, mad as it made me.

There are a couple of different reasons why people might send in a question via e-mail or a chat service while they're in the library. A simple one might be that they just don't want to get up and risk losing their computer, especially in a busy, highly trafficked area. (Yes, they might also be lazy, but that doesn't mean they shouldn't be able to ask a question and get an indignation-free response.) But it might also just tell you something about the way they perceive the current service. Maybe they think it's too public for a personal or embarrassing question.

Whether those perceptions are true or false is irrelevant for the moment (but if they're true, that service has a whole lot else on its plate beyond establishing a digital reference service).

Breaking Boundaries of Time and Space

What matters is that we now have an opportunity to provide direct, mediated services to people, breaking the boundaries of place and time that have constrained us (and our users) for millennia. This emerging environment for reference should be every reference librarian's fever dream: the chance to pursue more and deeper information needs, to do the kind of research and searching and investigation most of us got into this business to do in the first place, to do it well, and to help more people than we ever could before. It's breathtaking to think of the possibilities these technologies now afford us. So let's look in more detail at some of these matters technological in the next chapter.

QUESTIONS FOR REVIEW

- Is a response that doesn't cite a source, clarify the questions, and so on, necessarily "bad" or "substandard"? If the user is happy, what difference do these things make?
- Is there anything missing from the list of components of "mediation" (pages 74–80)? Which component would be most important in a digital environment? Which one is most uniquely the domain of the reference librarian?
- On resources—most library collections now are changing by the minute, with the incorporation of licensed databases and free Web resources. Does this imply we have to get *closer* to those sources and resources, know them more fully, and know what we've got more completely, or does it mean we have to keep a more distant, bird's-eye view to avoid being trapped in resources that evaporate or are no longer licensed or available?
- Are the kinds of guidelines developed by IPL, RUSA, and so on, for our benefit or for users? Do most users care about such things?
- Given all the potential benefits and problems, who should keep and have access to transcripts or records of digital reference transactions? For how long? Should anything be removed from them?
- Why hasn't Stumpers-L been more successful?
- Can collaborative digital reference services work?

ENDNOTES

1. See, for example, American Library Association, "ALA Office," for more information. Available at: www.ala.org/washoff/copyright.html.
2. Oxford University Press, "Better Writing: Email, SMS, and Online Chat." Available at: www.askoxford.com/betterwriting/emoticons/?view=.
3. These guidelines, and other information about the six-times-yearly award, are from the Virtual Reference Toolkit. Available at: www.vrtoolkit.net/greenaward.htm.
4. Carnegie Mellon University, "The Chat Reference Experience at Carnegie Mellon University." Available at: www.contrib.andrew.cmu.edu/%7Ematthewm/ALA_2001_chat.html.

REFERENCES

Janes, Joseph, and Chrystie Hill. 2002. "Finger on the Pulse: Librarians Describe Evolving Reference Practice in an Increasingly Digital World." *Reference & User Services Quarterly* 42, no. 1 (autumn): 54–65.

Chapter 4

Technology

In this chapter, we'll discuss

- technological options for improving reference services;
- how to recognize important features when evaluating technological innovations;
- key technical issues, including infrastructure, standards, design, glitches, authentication, and user profiling; and
- what technologically mediated reference will lead people to expect from library services in the future.

Now we'll get down to it. I imagine for a lot of people this may be what they're looking for out of this book. A few of you might even have turned to this chapter first, which I can certainly understand (though you've missed some good stuff—go back and read the rest sometime!). None of this is all that surprising, because so much of the recent discussion about reference work focuses on technological issues. "What kind of software do you use?" "Have you heard about a good use of chat?" "Isn't everybody going to 24–hour service?" And so on. Those are the kinds of questions people ask at workshops and conference sessions and on the listservs I read, and when you're putting together such a service, these are important questions to ask.

But they're not the only questions, as I've already discussed, and should not, of course, be the first or driving ones. I think it all boils down to this: the real question librarians are asking is, "What should I do?" I was going to save this until the end of the chapter, but I think it makes more sense here: there is no single, definitive answer to that question. The technological environment in question is far too volatile, and different institutions and communities will have very different needs and desires for a single, one-size-fits-all solution, despite what vendors will tell you. We've been through this before, when we converted from card catalogs to the digital kind and then converted again and again. Often, though, the technical-services side of the house largely drove those discussions. Now the shoe is on the other foot, and it's the public-services people who are trying to think about how most appropriately to fold technology into what they do on a daily basis.

In this chapter, then, what I'd like to do is walk through a few major technological options for reference work, think about what it is we really might want out of any technology, raise a few more issues specifically in the tech realm, and then finish up with some discussion of questions in a technologically mediated reference encounter.

As we begin thinking about this newest set of technologies to become part of reference work, it's worth reflecting one more time on the grand tradition to which they belong. Reference librarians have a long history of using and adopting new technologies to help them in their work, from telephone- and Teletype-based services in the previous century through a variety of mechanical or automated systems (manual co-occurrence indexes; CD-ROMs; early Internet work with Archie, Gopher, and so on). By its very nature, reference work implies facility with technology; reference librarians have always made sure that their work went beyond that to fluency and innovation, and it's exciting to watch and be part of their doing it again.

TECHNOLOGICAL OPTIONS FOR PROVIDING REFERENCE SERVICES

We've previously—although briefly—discussed some of the technological options that currently present themselves for reference work. Here we will consider them in more depth, looking at their advantages and disadvantages, mentioning some specific examples and features, and concluding with a notion of what the best kinds of options would offer.

Note, however, that I'm not going to spend a whole lot of time on specific systems or software. It's always risky to do that in any book that intends to have any shelf life at all; it's particularly perilous here, because this is such an emerging market, and many new players may enter in the not-so-distant future. To keep all of this from becoming obsolete the day after the book is published, I'll focus instead on general features and thoughts, which will be less immediately valuable as a buyer's guide but, I hope, of more use in the longer run.

E-mail

The first and simplest technology to consider is electronic mail. This is how it all started, really, with a few librarians realizing this was a good way to communicate not only with colleagues and vendors but also with patrons. In some cases, the patrons were there first, sending e-mail to any address they could find on a library Web site or bookmark, using it as a way to ask for assistance. In the very, very beginning, this was sometimes difficult, because for many libraries, e-mail was hard to come by. Since the free e-mail services, such as Hotmail and Yahoo! mail, have started, though, this has become a nonissue, and there are very few libraries and librarians left without some sort of e-mail available to them.

E-mail has some definite advantages as a reference tool. In addition to being easy to use and understand, it's the lowest common denominator. Not only is it possible to assume that almost every librarian has access to e-mail, but it's also possible to assume that many—but, significantly, not all—potential inquirers do as well. I've seen a couple of libraries with e-mail-based systems link directly to Hotmail or Yahoo! mail, suggesting that people set up free e-mail accounts to be able to use the service, a simple but effective idea. In general, an e-mail-based service is cheap (at least technologically speaking) to build and maintain.

Since e-mail traffic leaves traces, it's possible to keep copies of what was received and sent. These can be used to evaluate the kinds of questions received and how they're phrased, time taken to respond to questions, the quality and accuracy of the responses, and so on. It's also possible to use e-mail to send not only answers or brief quotations of print or digital materials but also files, which might include documents, the results of searches, URLs of interest, and so on. As we discussed in Chapter 2, the asynchronous nature of e-mail also provides that extra time to tackle difficult or challenging questions, compose responses in a thoughtful way, and take just a step away from the immediacy of the face-to-face reference encounter. It is also possible, of course, to use e-mail to respond to a question that is posed in person or over the phone; this can often be good for those same deeper questions and might yield substantially better responses for those people willing to wait a little while for a higher-quality answer.

However, I've always thought that e-mail provided a very thin connection, especially for an infrequent or inexperienced user or one who is unfamiliar with the library. There are none of the social conventions of the face-to-face encounter, so it's possible to send a question and then, when asked for clarification, never to respond, leaving the librarian to wonder what happened. Many people rightly point out that it's very difficult to conduct what we think of as a good reference interview strictly via e-mail, and the time lag in having any sort of multipart communication can mean that an answer to a simple question requiring clarification or refinement may take days. One more thing: if people are going to use e-mail, they have to be able to type, have access to a computer, be able to write and read—all of which may be obstacles to some potential users.

Web Forms

The close cousin to strictly e-mail-based services is the Web form. Largely, this is for the intake of questions; while it would be technologically possible to use the Web in responding (by, say, giving questioners a code number to enter into a Web form to get access to a response), the usual paradigm is the use of a Web form to solicit the question and e-mail to respond.

This use of the Web, then, shares most of the advantages and disadvantages of e-mail-based services. It does require access to a Web server, of course, which is more difficult and costly than simply using free e-mail accounts and also means somebody's got to run the Web server, maintain it, keep the pages fresh, check for broken links, and all the other required and necessary technical stuff. It also extends the reach of the service, meaning that more people can find it (assuming it's not impossible to find, buried under several layers of Web pages). I've already made my case about the effectiveness of Web forms as interview devices, so I'll spare you that again, but it's worth reiterating here that there is likely a sector of any library's community of service that would prefer this mode of communicating with the library staff for some information needs, and as such this mode may well be an important part of most, if not almost all, reference services.

Chat and Instant Messaging

Many libraries and librarians have been experimenting with chat and instant-messaging (IM) technology. While these aren't the same, strictly speaking they're close, so I'll discuss them together. There are a number of options here, from ICQ and instant-messaging tools from AOL and Yahoo! and MSN to a wide variety of chat applications. Some are very simple, Web-based tools that allow for quick communication; others are much more fully featured, allowing for customization and personalization, the capture of transcripts, the pushing of Web pages, and so on. All of these are similar, though, in that they are designed for back-and-forth, synchronous conversations, via typing of text, among two or more people. Some of the more advanced are also integrating voice and even video, via Web cam, into chat or IM sessions.

The use of this software has some intriguing potential advantages. They are relatively simple to use and have a large installed base, especially in some organizations and among many young people (particularly teenagers) who use them as standard communication tools. That kind of widespread use may make these particularly attractive for librarians serving communities of users who are already using these tools, used to them, and online a lot. Even for people who are not already users, they are relatively quick to learn (though not always immediate, thus perhaps not the best option for casual, one-time users). Transcript options might yield some of the benefits described above for e-mail traces. They are also synchronous, which means that interviewing may be more natural and more conversational than it is via e-mail or a Web form.

However, the bandwidth, metaphorically speaking, is often quite low. Absent the use of voice or Web cam, all you're getting here is text, possibly with a few smiley faces thrown in, but no non-verbal cues, and so the potential for misunderstandings and time-consuming clarification might be high. These still require typing, and in fact that typing is now more immediate, since the other person is waiting on the line, which is not the case with an e-mail exchange. This kind of ups the ante in ways, since this technology reinforces immediacy, but a slow typist can be very frustrating for the conversational partner. It turns out that accuracy in typing is not necessarily required—many chat conversations are filled with typos, misspellings, abbreviations, and so on, and more experienced users don't find that problematic at all, though I can imagine most librarians would find it hard to adjust quickly to that kind of world—and still feel like professionals, that is.

Chat and IM can also be really boring, especially when a participant goes away, and it doesn't take long for that boredom to set in. In a matter of a few seconds, people will start to get antsy and could easily drift away, psychically if not physically, and this may not be conducive to an intellectual exchange (like a reference encounter). There may well be a lot of potential in chat and IM, but I suspect it would be for specific, targeted niche audiences and communities.

Videoconferencing

While it's not currently used in any wide-scale way, at least as far as I know, it's interesting to ponder what the use of videoconferencing or something like it might be like. This would enable one- or two-way direct, visual communication, either allowing the inquirer to see the librarian or, with the right kind of hardware, allowing the two to see each other. In ways, this is just an extension of the Web-cam notion we discussed under chat and IM above, but there are a range of options upward from there, increasing in sophistication, bandwidth, image quality, and of course expense.

This would appear to resolve many of the concerns expressed about the reference interview. It's live communication that permits one or both parties to see those nonverbal things that are missed in textual interchange and allows for interaction to support the clarification of the nature of the inquiry, and it's likely that there are settings in which this kind of communication would be ideal. Here, the need to type would be no barrier and there'd be no lag, as there is with e-mail or Web forms. It also could help both librarians and users to feel that they're in a bit more personalized setting; it's not, of course, but it might be that just seeing the other person in a video window or on a screen puts some people at ease and makes them feel more comfortable.

It's also quite possible that it would creep them out. Being on camera can make some people quite self-conscious, and there might be lots of people who don't like the idea of staring into a camera, either to do reference or to ask a simple question. Also on the disadvantage side of the ledger: the lack of a textual transcript (shy of manually transcribing a video recording, which is incredibly time-consuming and tedious; speech-recognition software likely wouldn't help much right now) and, of course, the very large expense for software and, especially, hardware. High-end videoconferencing technology runs well into several digits to the left of the comma, if not more, and that would put this out of the reach of all but the largest or most technologically saturated environments.

This is an intriguing idea that probably just wouldn't work, and I'm not surprised that few, if any, libraries have tried it yet. I could envision such a service working in a corporate or government or organizational environment that already has video technology implemented throughout and is already using it for meetings or other functions. Piggybacking an information service onto an already existing set of uses for video technology might be a shrewd way of encouraging people to use that service, but otherwise I think video will be restricted to the Web-cam level for almost everybody else, at least for the foreseeable future.

Call-Center-Based Software

The other major technology that has received a lot of attention and that a large number of libraries have begun to implement is call-center-based software. This is really an adaptation of the kinds of programs used by customer-service centers for handling service requests via telephone or the Web. This market has exploded in the last year from a few experimental uses of systems such as Remedy to a number of offerings directed specifically at the digital reference world. LSSI, 24/7 Reference, CS-Live, Convey, Citrix—these are the names one sees at conferences, in ads, and on listservs. They vary in terms of features and functions, but the basics are the same.

What this software does is enable an operator (in our case, a librarian) to handle requests in an integrated way. Most provide for some sort of live interaction with the user, via a chat window most likely, and give the librarian a number of options for that interaction. Besides the chat, some of these packages allow for

- *scripts* to assist the process of communicating by allowing canned messages ("Welcome to our reference service. What can I help you with?" or something like that) to be sent instead of their having to be typed every time;
- *page pushing*, which is the sending of a URL to the user's

machine and having the page displayed in the user's browser window and is handy for showing the results of a search;

- *form sharing*, where both the librarian and the user see the same form and, as the librarian fills it in, the user is able to see how that's done—a potentially useful instructional tool;
- *application sharing* (I've also heard this referred to as *shadowing*), where both can use the same software package, such as a word processor or a spreadsheet;
- *co-browsing*, another term for much of the above and also called *escorting*, in which either party might take the lead in showing the other through a Web search, for example; and
- *evaluation* by sending a brief form—for example, at the end of an encounter—asking users for feedback on the response they got.

This terminology is still in flux and might well continue to evolve, but it's easy to see that a good number of the features of interest here take advantage of the synchronous nature of the interaction, trying to replicate or supplement what's possible in a face-to-face encounter around a browser window.

The obvious advantage of this kind of software is that it is (largely) designed for precisely this kind of interaction. I put *largely* in parentheses because in reality it's been adapted from more specific kinds of uses, and at least in the early days that genealogy made this software less than optimal. When you think of, say, a customer service selling clothes or providing technical support for hardware, the kinds of things these packages were originally designed for, there are similarities with reference work, but there's one glaring difference: both involve interactions between people asking for help and people trying to provide it, both permit people to communicate and share resources, but the domains are very different. If you're providing tech support, there are a lot of things you might get asked, but the large majority of those questions are predictable and, more to the point, repeated. You're not, for example, going to be asked how to fix a printer jam and then what the population of France was in 1572.

As a result, these packages were designed to deal with a relatively small set of potential questions and to store ready-made responses to them. (Moreover, many companies use their question-answering services as gauges of the quality of their documentation and help systems and view questions to these services as failures of their information resources. Contrast this with a lot of reference librarians who are proud of their statistics as measures of how well they're serving their population. Could it be that reference questions are indications of the *failure* of cataloging and indexing systems? Should we be happy about the perceived drop in reference questions—maybe people are doing better on their own, and isn't that a good thing, in general?)

Reference work, of course, isn't like that. Anything and everything can come in, and that kind of variety can choke a system that's predicated on a more restricted range of questions. The current packages are better, but in some small way their heritage persists.

In general, also, these packages are easy on the user, although some require users to download applications to support the chat or other functions, which isn't such a hot idea and is a potential impediment to use, especially by people at computers not their own.

On the other side of the coin, these packages are, in general, quite expensive, but large systems or cooperatives can share the cost. There is also a pretty steep learning curve for most librarians, not only on the use of the software itself, which can be kind of tricky, but also in doing reference this way, focusing on the use of digital and networked materials, conducting interviews in this medium, and so on. Done properly, this can be an effective and valuable way of serving users, but it won't come easy or cheap.

What Do Reference Librarians Really Want Technology to Do?

So, it's pretty clear that none of the above is perfect or without potential problems. But let's indulge in a little fantasy/thought experiment while we're thinking about this. What would be the important features or aspects of a technology or set of technologies that would be great across the board for most, if not all, situations? Well, it probably ought to

- be easy to use and understand, both for the user and the librarian;
- be commonplace or ubiquitous and easy to get at, especially not requiring any add-on or plug-in on the part of the user;
- provide high bandwidth—that is, allow for a great deal of interaction between user and librarian;
- allow for a high-quality, professional-level interview;
- permit user and librarian to make enough of a personal connection to yield a productive interaction;
- be free of time lag, unless either party desires it (to compose a thoughtful response, for example);
- allow the librarian and perhaps also the user to push information in some way;
- support evaluation of the service; and
- be comfortable and affordable on both ends.

Surprise—no technology yet satisfies all of these. And as situations and environments vary, some of these will be of greater or lesser importance. These might serve as some guidelines in thinking about, evaluating, and asking questions of vendors about various technological options.

PRACTICAL ISSUES RAISED BY THE NEW TECHNOLOGIES

Incorporating the use of new technologies such as these into reference work is going to make many things very different and raise lots of questions. In this section, I'd like to introduce some of these issues and work through them a little.

Infrastructure

First, and perhaps most obvious, is the question of technological infrastructure. It goes without saying that if a library reference service is going to start using e-mail or Web forms or chat or call-center technologies in its work, it's going to have to have the necessary hardware and software and the support for those to make it work effectively and correctly. For many libraries, this won't be a problem, but for libraries with small budgets, thinner current infrastructure, or quite ambitious plans, this will mean an initial outlay of money and time to get up to speed. This may involve upgrading current computers, buying new ones, adding new peripheral devices (Web cams, microphones, scanners, and so on), purchasing or licensing software, or integrating new software with current software (catalogs, databases, e-mail, campus or other local networking, and so on). That may or may not be cheap and may also require additional staff time, either internally or externally. There are also potential training issues here, which I'll discuss in the next chapter.

Technological infrastructure is not only a concern on the library's side. The required setup on the user's, or client's, side may be a concern as well. If the library uses software that assumes a particular kind of hardware or software on the client's side (say, software that won't work with Macintosh computers or with browsers other than Netscape or Internet Explorer), this may make it difficult or impossible for some users to get to the service or to use it fully. In addition, some systems require users to download applications or software or to accept cookies, which is also a potential barrier to their use. Again, depending on the nature of the users and the communities for which the service is being designed, these may or may not be important or problematic concerns. Libraries that can assume a particular baseline or set of technologies and software can take advantage of those assumptions in designing their services.

Collaborative Service Standards

The enthusiasm and excitement over collaborative services lead quickly to a concern about standards to help individual libraries work together. At present, there are no such standards; the QuestionPoint folks have developed a Web form for members to use in moving questions around, but this is a de facto standard only for the QP universe, at least so far. A discussion has been ongoing for quite a while now around a potential standard called QuIP (question-interchange protocol); Dave Lankes of the Virtual Reference Desk and Michael McClennen of the Internet Public Library, among others, have been working on this.

Standards in any environment are by their nature often complicated and involved; standards work here is no exception. There are a large number of pieces of information that could be represented in a question as it's being sent from one institution to another, not only to help in crafting a response but also in making sure it gets back to the correct user; allowing it to be stored and retrieved as part of a database of responses; recording the history of who has looked at the question, worked on it, and found potential sources for a response; allowing for multiple iterations or versions of it; profiling users and institutions for future reference; and so on. This work is ongoing, and recently the National Information Standards Organization (NISO; the folks who gave us Z39.50 and the like) has held a workshop and appointed Committee AZ to develop a national standard for question interchange.

Service Design

The design of the service, particularly the face that is presented to the public, is also important. We've had library Web sites for quite some time now, and any digital reference service needs to be tightly integrated within a library's Web presence to make it a seamless part of the library and to reinforce its centrality within the library. It also should be easy to find and clear and easy to use, and it should lay out its expectations and policies. Call it something obvious, like "Ask a Librarian" or "Get Help Now," or place it under a link marked "Can't Find What You're Looking For?" and put the link everywhere: on the front page, on every other page of the library Web site, even in the catalog and database pages if you can. Don't use jargonish names like "Electronic Reference Desk" (how can a desk be electronic?) or "Adult Services" (which we all know means something quite different on the Internet). I also generally dislike cutesy names like "Answer Express"; they really get in the way of people finding and understanding what is going on.

Since in many cases, it's difficult to assume much on the part of the user, I'd think a service would need to allow for users with all levels of technological sophistication and experience and a wide range of bandwidth. This doesn't necessarily mean lowest common denominator, but it does mean allowing people with very slow dial-up connections to use a service via e-mail or a Web form. There's no reason services like those can't be developed right alongside higher-end or higher-bandwidth services that might use voice or streaming video, if those are likely to be of use as well.

Home RefDept ReadyRef Business Career Community Health History Libraries Readers Spanish

KCKPL Adult Services/Reference Department

E-Mail Reference and Referral Service

What   When   E-mail Form

What is it?

The KCKPL online reference service allows you to send our library staff reference questions by e-mail. We can provide a brief factual answer to a specific question or refer you to materials that may be of help. We are not able to provide indepth research through this service. **Because of the complexity of genealogy research, we only accept these questions by regular mail.** All questions will be treated with strict confidentiality.

When should I expect a response?

Our Adult Services staff members answer these questions in addition to handling their regular duties. You should receive an acknowledgment of your question within 24 hours, but we may not be able to handle all the questions we receive in a day. All questions will be reviewed and those that are accepted should receive an answer or status report within 48 hours. For better service staff may in some cases reply with a request for clarification.

Our Reference Question Mailbox is checked once a day. Questions are read and reviewed, and accepted questions will be answered or referred to another staff person with more expertise in a particular subject area. Staff will respond with a brief factual answer or a referral to other sources that may be of help.

E-Mail Question Form

What is your name?	[_____] (required)
What is your e-mail address	[_____] (required)
Where do you live (city/state)	[_____] (required)

Type of answer preferred
      ⊖ Brief factual answer
      ⊖ Ideas for sources to consult for your research

Will you use this information for a school assignment?   ⊖ Yes ⊖ No

I won't need this information after (mm/dd/yy)   [_____] (required)

Tell us your question. Please use complete sentences and be as specific as possible. Tell us

Figure 4.1 Kansas City, Kansas, Public Library.

Figure 4.1 shows quite a simple but effective design, pointed to directly off the library's main Web page (as are the others shown here). This page demonstrates to me the power of a straightforward layout, one that would load quickly with a dial-up connection and conveys a lot of information without getting in the way. Great job.

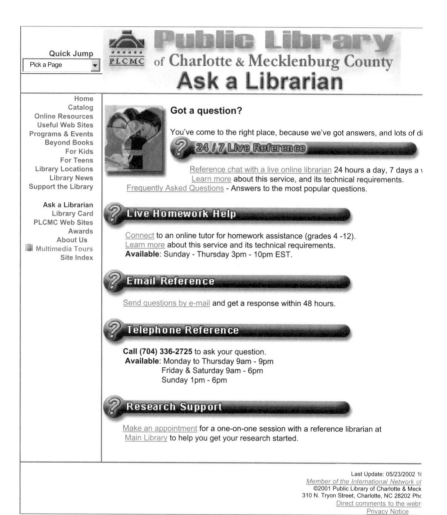

Figure 4.2 Public Library of Charlotte and Mecklenburg County, North Carolina.

Figure 4.2 shows lots of ways to get at the services. The page is nicely laid out, well integrated into the library's overall Web-site design.

YORK COUNTY LIBRARY
e-reference

Can't find the answer? Ask us!
The answer may be closer than you think.

Do you want to know if the library has a specific book?	Do you want to know if the library has a specific magazine or newspaper?	Do you want to reserve a specific book, video, audio book or CD?	Are you looking for assistance with Internet research?
Go to the online catalog and search by author, title or subject. You may reserve the item with your library card barcode number.	Go to the online catalog and search by title.	Go to the online catalog, search by title or author. You may reserve the item with your library card barcode number.	Go to the reference and research page, then look for your topic of interest.

If you cannot find your answer through this website, York County Library's electronic reference service may be of assistance. E-reference enables you to send a question via e-mail and get an answer via e-mail within a two business days. Use the form below to submit your question.

Questions
When asking for information, be as specific and complete as possible. We can answer only brief factual questions or suggest other places to look for the answer. We may not give financial, legal, medical or tax advice.

York County Library staff will attempt to answer genealogical questions. They will be subject to copyright laws and the following fees:

- **Labor:** $25.00 per hour
- **Photocopy:** $0.25 per page
- **Microfilm copy:** $0.50 per page

A letter will be sent upon receipt of a genealogy question. Acknowledgement

Figure 4.3 York County, South Carolina, Public Library.

Figure 4.3 shows how people with common questions are gently guided to the place where they can get help, the form is simple, the "Help Us Help You" statement is good, and the big question mark at the top certainly gets the point across.

Q*and***A NJ.org**

Powered by the
New Jersey Library Network

▸ About the Service

▸ Tips

▸ Disconnected?

▸ Participating Libraries

▸ Privacy Statement

▸ Contact

Connect

Don't search... Find.

We are a network of experienced New Jersey Librarians offering free live, interactive search assistance 24 hours a day, 7 days a week.

All you need to begin is an Internet browser
--
connect to a librarian now!

What kind of help do you need?

- **Search help on** *any topic:* — Connect me to me to a librarian now. Before you connect, please read our Internet browser requirements.

- **Tutoring help:** — Q and A NJ provides **free** live tutoring help for 4th - 12th grades through an alliance with Tutor.com. First-time users, please visit the Live Homework Help page. Return users, request a tutor now.

LIVEHOMEWORK**HELP**
Get live help
from real tutors now.

*— Need a **math** or science TUTOR? —*
*Use this **quick connect** shortcut*

- **School or class assignment** — Group and class "visits" to Q and A NJ must be scheduled in advance.

Teachers and educational media specialists should contact the service manager to make arrangements. **Click here** for more information.

Q and A NJ is a service for New Jersey residents and/or New Jersey-related questions.

Q and A NJ is designed to provide fast answers to your questions, using information found on the Internet and in proprietary databases funded by libraries. In most cases, Q and A NJ Librarians will provide an answer online in 15 minutes or less! If your question involves lengthy research, we'll get you started and/or provide a referral for you or your question.

Figure 4.4 Q and A NJ.org.

I love the headline in Figure 4.4, which inspires confidence and gets the point across. Lots of good information throughout here to help the user know what to do and expect, in a relatively simple design with a simple, nongoofy logo.

Glitches

Glitches. They always happen—usually when the boss or the board of trustees is visiting. They are inevitable, and we have to figure out what to do when they do happen. If patrons are at the desk or on the phone and something goes astray, we can ask them to wait, put them on hold, take a number and call them back, and so on. We'll develop similar sorts of mechanisms in digital environments: if a chat session suddenly evaporates and you have the patron's e-mail address, you can send a message to follow up. If you don't have an e-mail address, there may well be little you can do other than wait and hope the user tries to reconnect. If e-mail bounces, it's like a disconnected phone number, and again, other than trying to send the message again, this may be a lost patron and wasted effort. Servers will go down without warning, and other mysterious problems will crop up. We certainly hope that the software we use will continue to grow more robust and dependable and that problems like these will be minimized through training, experience, a more durable infrastructure, and so on, but we'll also develop good professional ways of dealing with the problems as we go. It's no use denying, though, that they'll happen.

User Authentication

An increasingly serious concern is the question of authentication of users, especially with the use of licensed proprietary digital resources. Here, library type likely makes a significant difference, at least in terms of what can be expected and done. It's likely that most academic libraries and probably many special libraries can assume that their communities are relatively used to authenticating themselves to get access to e-mail, intranets, library services, and so on, and may already be taking advantage of institution-wide authentication mechanisms. Getting those mechanisms to work together with digital reference services is the next step—relatively easy if it's a simple e-mail or Web form, more challenging as the level of the sophistication of the software approach rises. For example, my university library does a very good job providing access to all kinds of digital materials, making them easy to find, and so on, mostly through IP addressing and proxy servers.

But to authenticate myself to the library per se, to request materials or to see my circulation records, I have to give my bar code number instead of my university computing password and ID. I'm sure there are lots of good reasons why these authentication mechanisms don't yet interoperate, and I hope someone is working on it, but from a user's perspective, it's a pain in the neck to have to reach for an ID card to renew books. There are many questions to be asked of software vendors about interoperability on many levels, including authentication, but these are questions those vendors need to be able to answer.

Public libraries and probably most school libraries are in a different situation. Some public libraries currently ask, for example, for a library bar code number to be able to get remote access to licensed databases, and moving that mechanism over to a digital reference service looks much like what we discussed just above. But many don't, and they're going to have to make some decisions. Are they going to restrict their services (all or part of them) to just those who have library cards? If so, how will they enforce those restrictions, and what about people who are members of their service communities but don't have library cards? Will they offer different kinds or levels of service to people willing and able to provide authenticating information? Will they explore other mechanisms of authenticating (say, asking for a local address or phone number—these are less secure than library card numbers but at least are something)? And if they don't require authentication, how will they cope with licensing issues and restrictions?

All very good questions, and though these are raised in the context of public libraries, they cut across all types of libraries in one important way. We never asked these questions of people before, at least not from the word go, in a reference interaction. In face-to-face or telephone reference, we typically ask where users live or whether they are members of the community only if it is relevant, say, if the request is going to use library resources extensively or if materials need to be circulated or mailed or faxed or if we need to return a call. But it certainly isn't the first question out of the reference librarian's mouth, which is what an authentication method amounts to. If somebody presents herself or himself at a reference desk, we try to help first and foremost and worry later, if at all, about whether the patron is paying for the service (some private academic libraries and subscription libraries do require proof of membership to use the service, to be sure, but this is a small number overall). And, of course, if people are in the building, they have access to the full range of resources and services while they're in the building, as specified under most license agreements.

So here's the conundrum. We'd love to believe that digital reference is going to look like traditional reference in as many ways as possible. But it's clear that in this respect, it won't. If users are physically in the building (or, I guess, on the phone still), they'll continue to enjoy the privilege of full, unquestioned service in most respects. Once they cross the threshold (or fail to cross it, depending on your point of view), they're different, though, and will need to tell us who they are and, more important, demonstrate their financial support of the library to be able to use some resources and perhaps the service altogether. This is quite a different perspective on the reference service from the one most of us are familiar with.

And of course there's really nothing wrong with reserving the precious time of reference librarians and the use of costly information resources for people who are actually paying for the service in one way or another. In fact, it makes a lot of sense. But it's not the way we're used to operating, at least in most places, and so it will feel weird for a lot of people to work this way.

This will get even further complicated in collaborative environments. One of the pieces of information that might need to get included as questions get shipped around the world in cooperative services is what the users have the right to get at, based on where they live, where they go to school, and so on. If, say, a resident of Oneida, New York, asks a question of her local public library and the library forwards it somewhere else and Syracuse University tries to respond, the librarian at Syracuse is going to have access to lots more, and more specialized, resources and databases than the public library, but the patron hasn't paid for it. What does the librarian do, and how will she avoid getting in trouble with the vendor if it finds out and tries to enforce the license agreement? Moreover, how does the librarian in Syracuse know what Oneida's library has paid for? Add this to the mix—many resources are now purchased through consortium arrangements, some of which cross library types and provide a kind of web of permissions and authority—and you get a mess.

It might be easier than we think. It may well be, now or in the near future, that there's a baseline of services that a great number of libraries license (like, for example, WorldCat, ProQuest, *Encyclopaedia Britannica*, PsycINFO, and so on) and that many questions can be answered using those, perhaps not ideally but at least reasonably well, and that might reduce anxiety about this somewhat. But it's difficult to imagine these concerns evaporating entirely or soon, and practice will, once again, have to evolve.

DEEPER ISSUES RAISED BY THE NEW TECHNOLOGIES

In the previous section, I discuss some of the immediate concerns and issues that have come up with one or more of the technologies that are currently being used or discussed for reference work. Those are mostly practical or logistic issues, and they are important. But now I'd like to go a step further and think about some deeper things, a couple of which came up above, most of which didn't.

Profiling Users

For example, in the discussion earlier on standards, I mention the potential for profiling users in the course of shipping their questions around. This could be a real boon both for users and for services and harks back to days when reference work was local in nature and people knew their librarians and vice versa. To be sure, it was never completely like that, but even Samuel Green, in his 1876 article, mentions more than once using knowledge of particular members of his community in crafting responses to their questions, understanding their needs, and even suggesting resources for questions they hadn't asked yet. He knew—and librarians who have the luxury of getting to know individuals well know—their general preferences, who likes to get lots of things to wade through and who likes a specific answer, who speaks French or Japanese, and so on. In the hands of an experienced and trustworthy professional, that kind of metainformation about people and their needs can be invaluable.

But will people stand for it, especially in a time increasingly concerned with the privacy of personal and identifying information? People trust libraries and librarians (we hope!), but they may draw the line at telling us things like their preferences for information if the requests are mediated by the Internet and especially if those preferences are going to be shipped all over the world to other librarians. It's a shame, really; *we* know that we'd use this information in a professional and trustworthy fashion, but we might be in the minority. Not to mention that people might not be willing to sit still to tell us a lot of this kind of information to get a simple (or seemingly simple) question answered. Still, it's worth pondering.

A relatively simple idea, though one that would likely take more than a little work to implement, is enabling people to track the status of their questions, much the way FedEx or UPS permits the tracking of package shipments. Give each question a unique code number, and include a Web address when an acknowledgment goes out so people can see whether the question is being worked on, if it's been sent somewhere, perhaps even who is working on it and an estimate of the time it might take until a response is forthcoming.

Taking the Opportunity to Be Innovators

The use of the technologies we discuss here and the ones that will inevitably follow provides librarians with a tremendous opportunity to be innovators, to think ahead to the kinds of ways in which people will be interacting with information and then to plan to be there when those people need help. We already see huge numbers of people seeking information through Google and Yahoo! and their cousins, asking questions in chat rooms and with instant-messaging services and surfing the Web on handheld digital wireless devices of many kinds. How do we do reference there? What does a reference desk look like in a chat room? How do we help people when they're searching Google? How about when they're searching our own catalogs or licensed databases? What's the next technological plateau, and how do we get there first? These are not easy questions, and we may not be able to do everything, but I only hope that somebody somewhere reads these questions and thinks, Hey, we can do that. Is it you?

Encountering a New Generation of Questions

There has been considerable discussion, in these early days of digital reference, about what kinds of questions lend themselves to being asked and answered using these technologies. Some librarians say they'd prefer to handle only quick, ready-reference questions, often because they feel they can't do a reasonable reference interview in the digital world. Others think that this is the perfect opportunity to handle the deeper, more research-oriented queries, taking advantage of the chance to assemble a thoughtful response. Of course, much of this depends on the nature of the communities involved, the library, the technologies involved, and so on.

I'll just make a couple of general observations on this area. First of all, the overall technological environment in which we all now operate is likely already producing a change in the kinds of questions that will come to libraries, including a whole new generation of specific questions based on the technologies themselves. We've been dealing with "technological" questions for quite some time now ("How come this CD-ROM doesn't work?" "Can you change the toner/fix this paper jam/give me change for the printer/ help me unfreeze my browser/sign me up for an hour of computer time?"), but lots of librarians are discovering they now need to be able to respond to questions about matters more exotic: passwords, proxy servers, authentication, multiple database interfaces, policies, search techniques, printing, and on and on. I can't imagine this will lessen or change much in the foreseeable future, so we might as well get used to these.

24/7 Expectations

Second, the push for services that are always open (24/7 services, not to be confused with the service organization 24/7 Reference) raises the not unrealistic expectation on the part of users that the answers will come back really fast, if not instantaneously. This is not intended as criticism or as a plug for asynchronous-only services, but I know that if I were entering a question into a chat box or some other live mechanism, I'd be wanting and expecting an immediate answer. This significantly raises the stakes in many ways, and libraries that mount real-time, synchronous, live services are going to have to be able to back up those services with resources of all kinds to pull them off. This is not an impossible task, but I think this is worth thinking about very carefully before flipping the switch on a service such as that.

Now, if I had sent a question via a Web form or e-mail address, I probably wouldn't expect an immediate reply. I wouldn't mind if I got one, but my expectation would be that somebody would get back to me with a response to my question in a little while. The expectation is partly personal on my part but also largely based on my experiences with e-mail, Web forms, and synchronous services, and I would assume that many (but, significantly, not all) Internet users have had similar experiences and have similar expectations.

Matching Services with Expectations

Lastly, I believe that users of these services are going to be willing to accept the consequences of the environment in which they make their inquiries, especially if we tell them what those consequences are. A reference service using a Web form and e-mail that tells people they'll get an acknowledgment within three hours and an answer within 24 lets potential users make up their own minds about whether to use it. A Web-form-and-e-mail service paired with a chat-based service that gives an immediate answer but tells users that they'll only be able to get a quick answer to a quick question gives users choices so that they can make intelligent decisions about how and where to make their inquiries. Yes, I know, there are lots of people out there who would be challenged in making such an intelligent decision, and there will be lots of times when people will send deep research questions to the chat line and quicky facty questions via e-mail, but it wouldn't be hard to figure out ways of gently sliding them back and forth or suggesting the user call or stop by the library or whatever.

It is also virtually certain that these kinds of services will engender use by people we didn't traditionally serve in the past, people who wouldn't necessarily think of or bother to call or visit a library to get help on an information problem. We might well also lose people who won't or can't use technologies in these ways, but I suspect the number of people who are turned off by the fact librarians are now doing reference digitally and will thus stop using libraries altogether in person or by phone is insignificant. Of course, these are all empirical questions, and research and practice will help us to know better what happens as these changes emerge.

Matching services with expectations—those of both users and staff—will be an important component of the next generation of reference service development and work. That said, there's a great deal about reference work that is starting to shift and grow and change; I'll talk more about that evolution in the next chapter.

QUESTIONS FOR REVIEW

- How well established should a technology be before we adopt it?
- Should we bide our time and wait until the technology environment settles down a bit? Or should we perhaps get more involved, even develop new and necessary applications?
- Are reference questions *ever* an indication of the failure of our systems? Should one of reference work's goals be its own reduction in volume, traffic, importance?
- On page 133, I get back again to "What is the library?" Technology seems to pose this question repeatedly: how can we work to develop a clear and easily understood notion of "the library" that users and we can share?

Chapter 5

The Evolution of Practice and the Staff of the Future

In this chapter, we'll discuss

- how reference practice is changing;
- managing Internet-based reference services;
- developing and training reference staffs in a time of constant change; and
- staffing models.

The Challenge of Serving the Evaporating Patron

I had my first revelation that reference was changing in sometimes subtle and surprising ways after we'd had our first several months' experience in answering questions for patrons of the Internet Public Library. We began to notice that in many cases, we'd get an initial query from someone either via e-mail or via our Web form, and when we sent a follow-up e-mail to ask for clarification or help in understanding what was wanted, we'd get no reply. It took us a while to realize that this wasn't an isolated occurrence, and so then we began to think about what in reference librarianship we could use to deal with it.

And we discovered there really wasn't very much. In the "real world," if you have patrons who leave the library or hang up while you're in the middle of helping them, it doesn't take you long to figure out they're gone, and they often will tell you they're leaving. In such a circumstance, unless you know they're coming or calling back, it's over, and you don't have to pursue the question or worry about it much anymore.

In the digital world, that's not entirely true. Excepting the cases where e-mail messages sent back to questioners bounce (a different problem with a somewhat easier solution), if they don't respond, you can't be entirely sure they're gone. Perhaps they're just not reading their e-mail or perhaps they've already got an answer or no longer care. Or never cared very much in the first place. Or were just testing the service to see how long it would take. Or heaven only knows what else.

But there sits the librarian with a dilemma on her hands. Now what? Does she try again with a follow-up question and wait another day or two for a response? Does she try to guess and answer the question she thinks the person is really asking or should be asking or she can answer most easily? Or does she just give up and move on, hoping that if the questioner really does care, she or he will come back somehow? None of this is entirely comfortable or satisfactory for the type of person who's likely to be a reference librarian, and I'm not sure there's an entirely comfortable or satisfactory resolution to this issue. At the IPL, in general if no response is forthcoming, librarians will try to suggest a couple of general resources or ideas if they think they can make a good guess at the real question; if not or if it's simply unclear what's going on, the question is dropped.

It goes without saying that this same phenomenon happens in synchronous environments, perhaps even more perniciously. When users drop out of a chat or instant-messaging session, you're never really sure why—whether they had technical problems or got bored or found the answer somewhere else or what.

Managing Internet-Based Reference

The evaporating patron was the first of many intriguing and sometimes thorny challenges that cropped up in the course of starting a take-all-comers Internet-based library reference service. Taken together, they led to the guidelines for answering questions that I discuss in Chapter 3. Lots of libraries of all kinds have had guidelines for years for their reference services, and they helped largely to ration or apportion their services and resources. These guidelines would specify, for example, how long to spend on questions for different kinds of people (students versus faculty, community members or card holders versus others—assuming you could know that—and so on), whether someone at the desk would take preference over a phone call, who gets a database search and whether he or she has to pay for it, how to address patrons, whether a fax or e-mail was an appropriate response mechanism, and so on. I imagine most, if not all, of these policies are still in place, and they're quite valuable in delivering service.

In a digital domain, librarians seem to be inclined not only to extend those kinds of guidelines but also to augment them to discuss how to frame and phrase responses; when, if, and how to use licensed resources; whether a questioner is part of the library's service population; when to forward a question on to a collaborative service or transfer it from, say, a chat service to e-mail or an in-person encounter. That sort of evolution is natural, inevitable, and desirable.

And it reflects the myriad ways in which reference practice itself is evolving in this networked, digital environment. In this first part of this chapter, I'd like to work through several large categories of change and examine each in more detail to see what seems to be happening and what we might expect. In the second part, I'll speculate a bit on how we can help to prepare ourselves—and our successors—for some of the changes that we're experiencing.

RESTRUCTURING RESOURCE UTILIZATION

On this topic of resources, I think it's nearly certain that we'll see a growing reliance on digital resources of all kinds in reference work in general, especially in digitally mediated reference. That's not a surprise, but there's more here than meets the eye. Yes, certainly a lot of traditional resources—think dictionaries and encyclopedias—we all are used to in print now have marvelous adaptations in digital formats. (As do a few stinkers like almanacs, but we'll let that pass for now.) These fall into two major categories: things like the *CIA World Factbook*, which are virtually unchanged as they become digital, and others such as biography.com, which is effectively the old *Cambridge Biographical Encyclopedia* with extra material from the Biography Channel.

There are also great new resources that have emerged natively from the Web. My best example is the Internet Movie Database (www.imdb.com), which not only has the greatest, most elaborate search engine I've ever seen on a Web site but also has unbeatable content in the area of film; it's by far my favorite reference resource on film. It has two other intriguing characteristics. Pick any film you like, say *Young Frankenstein*, and click on "Awards & Nominations." You'll see there that, for example, Mel Brooks and Gene Wilder got Oscar nominations for Best Writing, Screenplay Adapted from Other Material. Fair enough; that's easily verified in all kinds of sources (but I'll bet not all of them will get the category name exactly correct, since the Academy loves to change those all the time).

But click on "Trivia," and you'll find out not only that the lab sequences were shot with the same equipment that was used in the 1931 *Frankenstein*, which many people know, but also that "the assistant property master's name, Charles Sertin, is on the third brain on the shelf" in the brain depository scene. OK, we're clearly in hard-core territory here, and this is partially explained by the comment at the bottom of this and almost every other IMDb page: "Errors and omissions on this page may be reported to the IMDb database managers by pressing the button below where they will be examined and, if accepted, included in a future update."

So a good deal of its authority and credibility rests in the users themselves and not solely in its editorial practices and publisher. And that publisher is the other interesting part of IMDb: amazon.com, which obviously uses it as a way to drive traffic to its video and DVD sales but, in my mind, doesn't compromise the quality of the content of the database at all. Fascinating—even more so if and when amazon.com gets into financial difficulty.

And we're even seeing what appears to be the renaissance of the individual as reference-work compiler, in the grand tradition of Poole and Webster and Bartlett. Web resources such as Who's Alive and Who's Dead (www.whosaliveandwhosdead.com) and Elections around the World (www.electionworld.org) are apparently one-person operations, and these individuals not only set the editorial policy (for example, Who's Alive covers only people the site maintainer cares about) but also claim authority and accuracy based on their time and interest and have no other basis—institutional or otherwise—to rest on.

Fitting Print into the Picture

So what about print? One of the intriguing questions around developing digital reference services, especially live, 24–hour services, is what, if any, kind of print collection to use. Some larger libraries have chosen to merge these kinds of services with dedicated phone-based services that already have separate print collections, thus allowing those collections to do double duty. Others have decided to dedicate very small print collections of the absolutely necessary things and rely mainly on digital resources. Still others have said they will use solely digital resources, to avoid the staff's having to run through the library's print collection to find resources. I think it's likely to be the case that print never vanishes entirely but that its impact will diminish over time. I doubt that many more print reference resources will be digitized—that period seems to be over—but more good things will be created in natively digital formats, as I discuss above. There's also the "they asked the question digitally, so they probably prefer a digital response" notion, which I largely subscribe to, but a digitally submitted question that can best be answered with a print resource ought to be answered with that print resource, unless it makes no sense or is completely unfeasible.

Moreover, more librarians will be more comfortable with digital resources in general. This is partially a technological and training issue but increasingly a generational one. This is hard to convey in writing, but I think there are two kinds of reference librarians, which I usually distinguish by gesture, so bear with me. Those in one group, mostly of my generation, when faced with a reference question, have an impulse to reach behind them, as for a trusty *World Almanac* or *Ulrich's* on a bookshelf. Those in the second, typically younger group have an impulse to reach for a keyboard, to do a Google search or use some other digital resource.

Neither is right or wrong, of course, but let's be honest: most of the shelf people are closer to retirement than the keyboard people, and more keyboard people are joining the ranks. This is natural and unsurprising, and they can do a really good job. Are they missing out on really cool and valuable stuff in the stacks? Yes. Are they ever going to know their print reference collections at anything approaching the detail of their more senior colleagues? No. Is that a bad thing? We'll find out. It's certain that they'll be more facile with the technology and resources (though I've known a lot of great librarians of a certain age who can make the Internet sit up and beg, so don't accuse me of ageism here), and that's probably appropriate for the environment and populations we'll be serving.

FAQ ASAP?

A few more observations in the general area of resources. I've seen a few, but only a few, examples of libraries mounting lists of frequently asked reference questions (FARQ) as part of their Web presence. There are many examples of policy- or technical-type questions ("How do I get a card?" "How do I renew a book?" "How do I use the catalog?" and so on) but not so many of the actual content-type questions ("What are the words that end in *-gry*?"—that sort of thing). There are a few good examples, and I know that the most frequently asked questions are of that first kind, but perhaps it's worth looking through that card file or list of the ones you get all the time, especially those that are locally or institutionally specific, and putting them up as a Web page to help people find those answers without having to ask you. Experience has shown, by the way, that it won't *prevent* people from asking those questions anyway, but at least somebody might find them useful.

Matching the Question with the Best Library to Answer It

One of the most important resources in any reference service, of course, is the staff, as I've said. Taking advantage of this digitally networked environment almost immediately takes us to the idea of working in cooperative ways. I've already discussed this more than once, but here I want to look at cooperative services from a practice perspective. The largest and best example at the moment is QuestionPoint, initiated by the Library of Congress and now supported by OCLC. QP is using a fairly complicated algorithm to automatically route questions to appropriate libraries based on a number of factors, including their capacity and current load, time zone and geography, and so on, but the largest and most important single factor is the subject area of the question (as assigned by the routing library using Library of Congress classification codes). Well, that makes perfect sense—if you've got a question in military history, you probably want a place like the U.S. Military Academy or the National Defense University answering it, as opposed to, say, a smallish public library. They've got the stuff and the staff to give good, authoritative, and timely responses, and they ought to get first crack at it.

In theory, this is a great idea. In practice, what it means is that libraries that play in this sandbox or others of a similar ilk may wind up increasingly specializing in those kinds of questions and subject areas. The University of Washington has strength in ocean and marine sciences. Let's say it starts to get a large number of questions in that area from QP and maybe other services, like a statewide consortium. Of course, they'll do well with those questions, and so perhaps the QP algorithm will favor them even more on that and will send along more questions. And so it goes, until UW has built up quite a bit of expertise on ocean and marine science digital reference. And the University of Michigan in Slavic studies. And Seattle University on comparative theology. Even though we normally think of subject strengths in an academic library context, presumably the same sort of effect could happen in public libraries as well.

These specialties wouldn't necessarily have to be by subject area; they could be by geography, language, and other characteristics, but it might well be an interesting side effect of collaborative reference work, especially when viewed against the discussions over the years about whether reference librarians were better off as generalists or specialists. What, then, would be the role of the generalist in such a world?

Using Experts as Resources

Staying with this thread, there are other resources that might become increasingly valuable. The use of experts who don't happen to be librarians but who are, say, on the faculty at these institutions or live in a particular community might help in working through difficult or detailed queries. We might also think about taking advantage of ask-an-expert Web sites and services, particularly those vetted and certified by services such as the Virtual Reference Desk. True, these folks won't bring the same attitude or experience to answering questions and often approach it more from the perspective of helping people know more about a subject area than from that of helping them understand and use information resources, but that doesn't mean we can't work together and take advantage of their expertise and subject knowledge. Of potential concern is also that such people or organizations might bring a particular point of view or bias to the table. In QP discussions, this has been the "what to do if the Tobacco Institute wants to join?" question. Two observations here: first of all, we've always been good at handling information resources that espouse a particular point of view, and second, sometimes the questioner wants precisely that point of view. I don't think there's anything particularly challenging here.

THE MORPHING REFERENCE INTERVIEW

The reference interview. Boy, I've heard more about this in regard to reference and how it's changing than probably any other aspect of the process. I won't revisit the whole screed on digital reference interviewing from Chapter 2 here, but I do want to make a couple of further related observations on the nature of reference practice in the interview. Recently, I did a workshop with an excellent group of librarians at a private university with extensive correspondence and distance-education programs. I began with a few general questions about reference work and then asked how they knew they'd done a good reference interview. They said that if the patron seemed satisfied with the answer, materials, and resources provided in the response, then the interview had gone well. I said that was OK, but how did they know that the interview had gone well *before* they began searching and compiling the answer?

That stumped them. After a little more discussion, they decided that if and when the language of both the patron and the librarian converged, that was a good sign and that nodding and agreement were good, and eventually we got to whether it was a good tactic to restate the query and ask the patrons if that was what they had in mind. These are good, of course, but I was struck by how difficult it seemed to be for these obviously experienced and talented reference folks to separate the interview from the response and the rest of the reference process. In retrospect, it's not that surprising, because the interview has always been seen as integral to the process, and of course when working with someone, there's often a back-and-forth aspect—an initial interview, finding a few candidate resources or answers: "No that's not exactly what I want." "Oh, here, what about this?" "Yes, that's much better." "Can you find me something a little more historical?" "How about this?" "That's exactly right." We're used to this process; most of us are comfortable with it and good at it—and in the digital world, it might be a lot less common.

This is especially the case in the asynchronous version, but even in a synchronous environment, I suspect there is a more marked division between the interview phase of a reference encounter and the search-and-response phase. It may be a hybrid, more like working over the phone than working in person; but with the kinds of technological demands of a chat or call-center session (juggling multiple windows, trying to move quickly so the patron doesn't get bored and leave, pushing pages, and so on), there is a greater pressure to get the interview over with and move to the answer than is typical on the phone. In an e-mail or Web-form environment, the interview is almost entirely compartmentalized, and thus the pressure is really on getting a solid understanding of the nature of the need from the first encounter, especially given the frequency with which people don't respond to follow-up questions and the necessary time lag involved in getting those responses.

We know a few things about doing a reference interview well using a Web form, and I discuss many of those ideas in Chapter 2. We know a lot less about how to do it well in a synchronous environment, and this is largely because we haven't been at it very long. It took us a while as a profession to get good at the reference interview in the first place, and what we did learn was almost exclusively a result of doing it a lot as opposed to its being the result of any serious research or investigation in this area. The only way to find out how to do a good chat interview—assuming one can do a good chat interview, and I think it's likely one can— is to have lots of people do lots of them, learn what works and what doesn't, and then share that knowledge via publications, presentations, workshops, and the like. But just because we don't know how to do it now doesn't mean it can't be known, and it certainly doesn't mean we shouldn't be trying such services to find out.[1]

I'd like to believe that there's a good way to do a reference interview in a technologically mediated environment like chat or instant messaging. And if there's a way to do it, I have confidence in talented and creative reference librarians' finding it out. It is possible, though, that there isn't one. It's possible that using chat and instant messaging and, for that matter, e-mail and Web forms and all these other technologies provides consistently less good interviews (however we measure that) than face-to-face or phone encounters do. If that's the case, we face a choice: abandon those technologies based on their shortcomings or live with them and use them to their best advantage and supplement them as best we can with better methods. Obviously, I'd favor the second approach, but some may disagree with me. As with many things, we'd have to balance the pros and cons of these, weighing the potential value of reaching more people with an inferior set of tools against serving fewer people better but making them call us or come in. We'd have to go back to our fundamental values to help us make that decision—and make some hard choices, no doubt.

And then there's the matter of time. Most reference folks are used to doing what they do in real time, interacting with the person asking a question either face-to-face or over the phone. Reference by mail, apparently not uncommon in the mid-twentieth century, has almost entirely faded away. I think this familiarity with the give-and-take of reference to date is part of what lies behind the allure many librarians feel for live, synchronous digital reference services such as chat and instant messaging offers the public. It's also more technologically sexy in its own way and more attractive for an on-the-go community, but I think for a lot of librarians it appeals to their sense of the way reference is done and thus seems a more natural way to proceed in thinking about developing and delivering services to a more digitally connected public.

None of which I disagree with. But either kind of digital reference, synchronous or asynchronous, will have an effect on practice in sometimes subtle ways based on the different ways in which time comes into play. For example, in a synchronous service, we will have the opportunity to engage the questioner in a dialogue that will feel more like what we're used to in the reference interview. But unless and until we have two-way video and audio linkups, which I think will be expensive and unlikely for most domains in the near future, that communication will be entirely via typed text and thus quite different in important ways.

Bringing Dead Time Back to Life

People get impatient with chat, especially experienced chat users. They can drop out of conversations because of technological problems or because they're just bored, and there are fewer social impediments to doing that than there are in the real world. As a result, librarians feel rushed and pressured to come up with responses quickly, if for no other reason than to keep questioners on the line and entertained. Many libraries using call-center-based software packages push pages specifically for this reason: to reduce the number of people who disconnect while the librarian's still looking for resources. This could, in less experienced hands, lead to lower-quality responses based on the perceived demands of time. Many libraries have also developed canned messages, to save time in typing frequently used phrases, such as "That's a good question; let me go see what I can find. I'll be back shortly." Those are a great idea and a real timesaving device, but they will have to be developed with some care to avoid their sounding like the kind of maddeningly robotic responses heard in voicemail hell.

Another good approach for dealing with dead time in a chat or live interaction is to estimate how long the search might take. That's an imprecise art at best, as we all know, so we'll have to get better at it if we're going to use it, but telling users that you're going to need about ten minutes or so (an eternity in an instant-messaging environment) will at least let them know what is likely to happen and give you a little breathing space. I'd overestimate the time I think I'd need, but not by a lot; longer times turn off more people, and if you do finish early, they might be away from the keyboard and thus you'd have to wait, which wouldn't be efficient on either side.

The kind of patter we're used to delivering in person—those descriptions and instructions we give as we're leading people back through the stacks to look at resources or as we're searching on a computer ("Well, let's start with Google, which is my favorite search engine." "I think we might find something useful in ERIC; do you know that? It's really the best database for educational resources." "You know, I think he might well be in *Who Was Who*, which is where you'd find dead British people.")—is much harder to do online. First of all, you have to type the whole thing, and second, if you start telling people about a resource or approach before you try it and then it doesn't work, I think you look more like an idiot than you do when it doesn't work in person—that's my guess based on the thinner personal connection we have in a digital environment. That's going to mean that more of these kinds of responses are likely to be self-contained, telling people only about what you actually found that was useful, which will have the unintended side effects of not showing them the totality of the search process or the other sources you considered and your decision-making process and thus also giving somewhat less of an opportunity for an educational component in the answer.

The Time-Lag Drag

Of course, there's a time lag in an asynchronous environment as well, and it's typically much longer. When someone sends in a question by e-mail or using a Web form, it could be quite a while, depending on time of day, available staff, and scheduling, before anybody reads it. Perhaps then it gets forwarded to an appropriate staff member to answer it, or it sits in a common in box waiting for somebody to take responsibility for it. Then if, heaven forbid, it needs clarification, a question will have to go back to the user and a response awaited. Time is clocking up here, maybe quite a lot of it, and for some questions this makes absolutely no sense at all. For others and, specifically, for some users, this may be the best way to interact with them: at their convenience and when pace isn't an issue.

There are ways in which canned responses could be used in an e-mail environment, and they can be attractive as well, to save typing. Because there's a lot of typing here, as there is in a synchronous service. Here, that typing can be done somewhat at leisure but also has to include everything about process, search, citation of sources, and so on, so there will generally be more text. In either case, users will have an artifact to go away with—the e-mail message or the transcript of the chat conversation (for those systems that make those available or easy to get at)—which they can consult later if they want to, a significant improvement over the entirely ephemeral nature of in-person services.

I've noticed something interesting in my own in-person practice, and it's based entirely on e-mail-based digital reference experience. In more than a few instances, when faced with a particularly tricky or involved question at the reference desk, my mind will run in several directions at once, and what I want more than anything else right then is time. I've grown used to having the luxury of that kind of time from answering questions via e-mail in the IPL's service, and I'm loath to give it up. And yet there's a person in front of me expecting a response right now. I don't want to look stupid or ineffective, so what to do? Here's what I've devised: I park the questioner for a few minutes by giving her or him something to look at, and my resource of choice for this is the *Statistical Abstract of the United States*. Why that? Well, to be honest, the first time I did this, it actually made sense for the question I was working on, but then I thought about it, and I think the *Stat Abs* are perfect for this. As we know, they're nearly impenetrable to the untutored and yet look as though they might be of use for almost any sort of query. I have found that by the time people have worked out (a) what it is, (b) how it works, including the fact that the stupid index refers to the *table* number and not the *page* number (which I have always detested), and (c) that it contains nothing of use to them, I'm right back there with a few ideas and resources and perhaps even an answer. Cool, huh?

OK, so I have to admit this isn't a particularly original idea; as I said, many call-center services do this with Web sites, and I'm sure other reference librarians have been doing similar things for years, but for me, this is my first example of how my reference practice can evolve based on adding these new modes of working with people. Much of digital reference practice (it's tempting to say, too much) has been drawn directly from what we've done in person, but it can also profoundly influence more familiar ways of doing reference.

In either real-time or e-mail-based services, there can be a virtual line of people asking questions or waiting for responses. In an in-person setting, people can see the line and how quickly it's moving and make up their own minds whether to join or stay in it based on how badly they want or need an answer. It's harder over the phone—you might get a busy signal or a continually ringing phone or be put on hold, which tells you it's going to be a while, but you don't know in advance whether you're likely to have to wait or for how long.

Those lines exist in digital services as well, but it's even harder for a user to know whether one exists and how quickly it's working. There might be technological methods for coping with this, such as call-center software that automatically gives an indication of current volume of use, expected wait times, and so on. E-mail-based services might give expected or guaranteed times for responses. We might also think about providing people with a tracking number to use to check the status of their question; this might be especially useful when a question has moved into a collaborative or networked service.

There's a trade-off here. Synchronous services typically yield quicker response times, but the pressure of time can lead to perfunctory or superficial responses. Asynchronous services can take much longer to produce responses, but those responses might be based on more thoughtful queries and better-composed responses. Some of these effects are due to our relative inexperience with these methods and technologies and might well become less pronounced as we learn more and get better at them.

It also might be the case, though, that these ways of working are more suitable for particular kinds of needs and questions, users, communities, and librarians. Some people may always want quick service and thus turn to chat. Some librarians may find they love instant-messaging or call-center services and put the bulk of their effort there. Some kinds of questions and needs might be best addressed in a more elaborate and less time-compressed way. To be sure, we'll learn more about these differences and idiosyncrasies as we do more of this, but the better we design our services, especially by telling potential users what works best where, the better the service we'll be able to provide overall.

STAFF DEVELOPMENT IN TIMES OF CONSTANT CHANGE

There's an easy, stereotypical way to think about staffing issues, particularly who's going to do reference and how: younger librarians (keyboard people) are going to be better prepared to work with new technologies and to thrive in a technologically saturated environment. Older librarians (the shelf people) are more experienced, know more resources, have a better feel for their communities.

Like all stereotypes, this has its elements of truth and can serve as a shorthand way of thinking about staffing issues. It also has substantial shortcomings; there are plenty of experienced librarians who are embracing new technological opportunities and leading their organizations in ways of thinking about providing new services, and there are lots of new librarians who have a solid background in the print culture and know the differences between the *Oxford English Dictionary* and the *American Heritage*. Minorities on both sides, I'd suggest, but not insubstantial ones.

I think there are several important considerations in building the staff of the future to take on the challenges of the digital world, and we'll look at a few of them here: training, staffing models, and the transition of existing staff.

Training for Tomorrow

Training has been much discussed over the last couple of years, and it's undeniable that there are things we all need to learn to prepare ourselves to give effective, high-quality service. The library profession has done a very good job in bringing itself up to speed on the functioning and use of the Internet. I have found that 95 percent of reference librarians responding to a survey say they've had Internet training in their degree program or in a current or previous position (Janes, 2002), but there's still much to be done. Ross and Nilsen also find that many librarians discussing the Internet in reference encounters seem to think and talk about it as a separate institution or even, in their words, an "alien space" (2000). It's fervently hoped that those days are leaving us quickly.

Now, though, we need to think about more focused training that will be of specific use in the digital reference world.

Mary Ross, the director of human resources at Seattle Public Library, posted the following message to the DIG_REF listserv early in 2002 on behalf of a group working on a statewide collaborative virtual reference project in Washington State. It makes an interesting and valuable starting point for consideration of training issues:

> The Washington State Virtual Reference Project is identifying the staff skills, abilities, and aptitudes that lead to effective virtual reference services, as a preliminary step in designing training.
>
> For purposes of this project, "Virtual Reference Service" includes all electronic methods by which libraries fulfill customers' information needs: e-mail, online forms, interactive chat and Web-browsing software.
>
> Here is a list of the skills, abilities, and aptitudes which the Training Committee developed:

1. Ability to derive professional satisfaction from virtual reference transactions.
2. Keyboarding proficiency.
3. Online communication skills and etiquette, for chat, e-mail and other online communication.
4. Ability to conduct an effective reference transaction in online environments, including the creation and use of pre-scripted messages.
5. Internet searching skills, in particular the ability to choose the best starting points for online searches.
6. Ability to effectively search, and demonstrate searching of library databases.
7. Ability to assist online users in developing critical thinking skills in locating, using, and evaluating information.
8. Ability to effectively conduct a collaborative browsing session with a patron.
9. Evaluation of online reference transactions, and identification of improvement strategies.

10. Multi-tasking and managing multiple windows; effective use of Windows keyboard commands and shortcuts.
11. Technical troubleshooting skills and ability to explain technical problems to IT staff to facilitate diagnosis and solution.
12. Ability to apply reference transaction policies in an online environment (e.g., time limits, obscene callers, harassment).
13. Commitment to continuous learning and motivation to improve skills in all areas of reference services.

(Before I go any further, I should say that I have a lot of respect for Mary and the other folks working on this project, which I hope, by the time you read this, will be up and running and a big success. I have served on the steering committee of the project from the beginning but had nothing to do with drafting or evaluating this statement. No real conflict of interest, so far as I can tell.)

It seems to me that this list breaks down into four categories. A few of the points (5, 6, 11, and 13) don't really have much, if anything, to do with digital reference so much as they have to do with reference in general, and I hope that all reference librarians have these skills regardless of the nature of the encounter. A couple (2 and 10) are purely technical—important in this realm but also more broadly and don't have much to do with professional skills.

The more interesting ones remain. Two are very specific to the digital reference world: item 3, on online communication skills, and item 8, on collaborative browsing. Neither of these has likely come up in anybody's graduate program (and it's an interesting question whether they ever will or should), but both are decidedly important. I think item 8 in particular covers a lot of ground, and we have a great deal to learn about what exactly it really means to "effectively conduct a collaborative browsing session with a patron," but I imagine we will learn soon enough.

Turning Existing Skills into Online Skills

The final and largest group consists of several points (items 1, 4, 7, 9, 12) that discuss translating existing skills into the online environment. Conducting the transaction online, instructing online users in information-literacy skills, evaluating online reference transactions, applying appropriate policies online, and deriving professional satisfaction from online transactions—again, I hope that all reference librarians can do these things, but their presence on this list would seem to indicate that it's not immediately obvious how to do them in the digital world, even if they are being done successfully now.

I think Mary and her group are right on this score. Many of these can be taught, online or not, but mostly these are things that need to be *learned*, through experience, mistakes, successes, and practice. But none of them is a direct translation (perhaps *transliteration* is a better word) from familiar reference practice. The ways in which we will evaluate ourselves and one another or help people think about their searching or interpret policy will not be exactly the same as the ways in which we do them now. They will, to be sure, be strongly flavored by current practice, especially for those with more experience, but we shouldn't expect or even want them to be slaves to what has gone before at the expense of deriving and learning new ways of thinking about and doing reference work. Thus, I think the point this group makes is that it's a combination of the old and the new, the technological and the professional, that will increase the performance of individuals and services.

Is there anything else? A subsequent posting on DIG_REF remarked on the importance of understanding appropriate uses for licensed databases and other proprietary resources and the need to cite sources and maintain objectivity and accuracy. I'd add these to the group's adaptation category.

A Call for Criteria?

It seems, though, that a lot of librarians almost want there to be more, some specific list of criteria or competencies or resources

or "Things To Know to Be a Good Digital Reference Librarian."
Proposals have been discussed (if not yet floated) for concrete digital reference training sessions and for criteria for some sort of certification, perhaps even formal certification, of competence to do digital reference.

This is an intriguing idea; we don't often find this in librarianship, other than in state certification requirements for school librarians. I have to admit I kind of like the general idea, and not really because it has anything to do with digital reference per se; what I like is the notion that we might lay out a body of knowledge and perhaps experience that we would all agree makes somebody a good, capable reference librarian and then certify that particular people and, for that matter, particular services meet those standards. Just having an ALA-accredited master's degree clearly doesn't do that—trust me, I've got one, and I'm not sure a lot of libraries want me on their staff. But this sort of certification by specialty or training works well in a lot of other professions and is an idea well worth pursuing.

I don't think, however, that there is now or will ever be a substantial set of "Things to Know" that will be solely of use in the digital world and not of use elsewhere or based on what we've done before. There will certainly be a mix of the new and the old, the technological and the informational and the interpersonal, and it may bear some resemblance to the list above. But it's not just about the technology or the environment, a point worth making in general.

Successful Staffing Models

In addition to figuring out how to prepare ourselves individually to do digital reference, we also need to figure out staffing models that will make services efficient and effective. One could imagine all sorts of ways of thinking about this, and I think most of these have been tried at least somewhere. Should people do digital reference while they're staffing a reference desk, in their off moments but also with access to print collections, or should they be somewhere separate so as not to be interrupted? When will these services be in the highest demand and thus require the greatest staffing? What kinds of information resources (especially in print) will be needed right at hand?

Naturally, responses to these questions are best decided at the level of an individual service, but the prevailing wisdom at present seems to be that trying to do digital reference work in off moments at the desk does everybody involved a disservice: the "live" patrons you're trying to serve, online patrons whom "live" people can't see and so wonder why you're distracted, not to mention you, the poor librarian trying to juggle all of this. Take it somewhere else—to an office, a dedicated computer somewhere, an already existing telephone-service area—but get it off the desk. And most people can't stand more than about a couple of hours at a time, so don't schedule people, even the most zealous of digital reference fanatics, to spend the whole day on a chat line. If you need access to specialized print materials, tell synchronous patrons you'll be gone for a bit; just walk out and get it if you're on e-mail; or decide that questions needing those kinds of resources have to be dealt with by people nearer to them, and move the question to the phone or desk service. This notion is reinforced by much of the literature on telephone and correspondence reference of the early and mid-twentieth century, which stresses the value of separate divisions for these kinds of services.

Opportunities for Innovation

Opportunities for innovation come up here in a couple of places. First of all, digital services provide the chance for people to telecommute. If the bulk of your resources are available remotely, then it really doesn't matter where the person answering the question is, including at home. It might also be worth investigating the use of contract, part-time, retired, or freelance reference librarians who want to work at home, maybe for several libraries, respecting the individual policies of each and focusing on resources their communities have available.

This idea easily extends to cooperative services of the type we've discussed in several places. I'd just add here the advantages that time zones can offer; as this is written, Cornell University and the University of Washington are working together on a real-time service, Cornell taking early-morning hours and Washington, those later in the day. (I have a couple of friends at the University of Hawai'i; institutions in time zones several hours ahead of or behind those of the continental United States might decide this is a chance for them, but I'd hate to seem them get overwhelmed.)

There are lots of potentially competing factors here, depending on the nature of the service any individual institution wants to provide for its community, and contradictions will obviously have to be resolved; these seem the right kinds of questions to think about while designing those services, though.

One of the more delicate matters at play here is the transition of staff, helping people with lots of experience adapt their skills to a new way of doing things. This kind of technological transition is always potentially dicey, and of course our technical-services and cataloging colleagues went through a similar process 20 years or so ago, when OCLC and shared cataloging changed their world radically. So now it's our turn.

Matching the Best Librarian with the Right Reference

There's actually an even deeper and somewhat overlapping issue at work here. It's not just a question of helping everyone on a given institution's reference staff to work in a digital environment. What we are likely to find, in trying to accomplish that or something like it, is that there are some people who are just naturally better at digital reference than others. No shock there, but of course we don't yet know who those people are or how to find it out, at least not yet. It may well be that the best reference librarians will be good regardless of medium, which would be straightforward enough. The more complicated (and more intriguing) scenario is that some people will be better at face-to-face, some better at telephone, others better with e-mail, and perhaps others still better at chat, instant messaging, video, call center, and so on.

This begs the question of what "better" is and how we measure it; I'll deal with that more in the next chapter. At the very least, though, there might be people who are better suited to different modes of work, more comfortable with them, and more likely to find success and fulfillment by using them. We all know that there are reference librarians who know a lot about sources and searching and can find things nobody else can find but can't do a reference interview to save their lives or just aren't very good with people. They do an OK job, but only half a job, and often leave people with the right answer and a bad aftertaste and turn them off returning. (One wonders if this is part of what underlies the cleft in the reference-evaluation literature—the continuing battle between whether we should evaluate reference performance based on accuracy or on the patron's satisfaction and willingness to return.)

Some of these people might be great at digital reference. Perhaps removing the interpersonal from the mix might unlock their potential, allowing them to take best advantage of their skills and knowledge and to use it to provide high-quality service to people whom they don't have to look at or talk to. Conversely, there are a lot of reference folks who got into the business precisely because of the interpersonal interaction and who thrive on it. I gave a talk a while back to a group about digital reference, and one woman in particular was visibly agitated at the prospect of answering questions via a keyboard and mouse as opposed to in person. She was nearly frantic at that notion, and I told her in response to her questions that I thought in-person work would always be around, at least in most places and for the foreseeable future, which calmed her somewhat, but she did not like this idea one bit. She and people like her would likely wither or at least be unhappy in a purely or even primarily digital environment, and so they probably shouldn't do it.

What's wonderful about this new set of technological options is that they are options—and will allow us not only to serve people in the ways they wish to be served but will also allow librarians to work in ways they find comfortable and rewarding. This seems like a win all the way around to me.

It would be very nice indeed to think that newer and older librarians will be working together to use a wide variety of techniques and experience on behalf of their users and communities. There are lots of experienced people with great ideas and initiatives who will continue to be terrific reference librarians regardless of the environment in which they work. There are also many, I imagine, who feel unprepared and believe they are watching the profession they cherish and spent a lifetime preparing for and learning about slipping away from them. I'll bet they're petrified and that their fear is manifesting itself as resistance, foot dragging, negativity, and other unpleasant things. We desperately need their wisdom and guidance to help us move our profession successfully forward, and those of us embracing these new ways of working need to do as much as we can to help our more skeptical colleagues to be valued, willing, and joyful participants. We cannot, though, permit that skepticism or doubt to overtake the good work that is going on; reference must continue to evolve and grow, or the handwriting will very clearly be on the wall.

In the end, what will happen here is that some set of reference practice will evolve. We certainly want to be able to take advantage of what has gone before, as I've said, but I don't think we want to be captives to the past either. In some ways, I think many people are trying too hard to make this new kind of work look a lot like what we have already done and known. That's a natural response—and the earliest services, IPL prominent among them, did a lot of replication of common reference practice. But if we spend too much time and effort (and money and technology) simply trying to "automate" the reference process, we may find that we will miss other opportunities and thus create add-on services that don't really serve as best they can.

The central challenge here is to decide, in a professional, principled way, what we should continue to do, what to add, and what to discard. That challenge can only be addressed by continuing to try lots of combinations of new things and doing research into what works and what doesn't. Perhaps we will discover, years from now, that what we're doing now is leading us toward something that resembles current reference work but is different in important and exciting ways. Perhaps it will even have a different name. Whatever it is, I hope it serves our various communities and users as well as reference work has over the last century and more.

QUESTIONS FOR REVIEW

- In addition to the "disappearing questioner," are there other examples of areas where traditional practice breaks down, doesn't help, or even interferes with digital approaches to reference?
- Will an increasingly digital focus change the relative importance and roles of generalists and specialists in reference work and in librarianship in general?
- Could (or should) there be certification of digital reference work, based on a standard body of knowledge, skills, and abilities?
- What does it mean to be "better" at digital reference than at traditional modes?
- Are we describing (or inventing) a different kind of librarian here or even a different profession altogether?
- Perhaps most pertinent, is this "reference" as we all recognize it? And if not, can this profession ever enthusiastically approach or embrace these ways of working?

ENDNOTES

1. I would note in passing here again the eye-popping study by Ross and Nilsen on the reference interview in practice, which finds that about half of the time it's not even done, let alone done well (2000), which in fact follows a substantial thread of research with similar findings (see, for example, Lynch, 1978). I'd take a lot more serious notice of the "we can't do a decent reference interview digitally so let's not do it" complaints if I was more confident that we were doing a consistently bang-up job of interviewing people face-to-face—or even *doing* the interview face-to-face.

REFERENCES

Janes, Joseph. 2002. "Digital Reference: Reference Librarians' Experiences and Attitudes." *Journal of the American Society for Information Science and Technology* 53, no. 7 (May): 549–66.

Lynch, Mary Jo. 1978. "Reference Interview in Public Libraries." *Library Quarterly* 48, no. 2 (April): 119–42.

Ross, Catherine Sheldrick, and Kirsti Nilsen. 2000. "Has the Internet Changed Anything in Reference? The Library Visit Study, Phase 2." *Reference and User Services Quarterly* 40, no. 2 (winter): 147–55.

Chapter 6

Making It Work: Creating and Institutionalizing a Service

In this chapter, we'll discuss

- major points to consider when envisioning an information service for a particular community of users and its needs; and
- a ten-step planning process for introducing a new reference service.

I think the most important word in the title of this chapter is also the longest. I've been continually impressed over the last several years with the creativity and originality of a lot of libraries and librarians and the services they've put together, often with the equivalent of chewing gum and baling wire, to try to extend their reach. That work has been commendable, we've learned a lot from it (good and bad), people have been served who wouldn't have been otherwise, and libraries are in general better for having taken on that work.

Where I think we haven't been as successful—yet—is in weaving those experimental services into the larger fabric. Many of the things people have done are incremental, often taking additional hours here and there, working outside the mainstream of the rest of the reference service or department. That's certainly understandable—experiments often start out that way—but it also means that digital reference services are vulnerable, potentially the first to go when the money gets tight and, worst of all, not seen as part of "real" reference. To many librarians, digital reference is different, even foreign; they might even see it as interesting and worthwhile, but until it becomes seen as a natural and indispensable part of reference work in general, it could easily always be seen as the poor stepchild and thus never given the resources and attention it needs to be truly successful.

In this chapter, I want to lay out some ideas on how to think about planning a service, make some suggestions on necessary features to consider, in some cases offer some options to contemplate, and then finish off with a checklist of questions to ask as you move through the planning, implementation, evaluation, and refinement stages.

Notice, as we begin, that I don't present this as a one-shot deal. It's not. Mounting a service is a large undertaking and should be approached that way. There's nothing wrong with the kind of experimentation we've seen, as I describe above. Without those early attempts, we wouldn't be where we are today with the kind of interest and activity we see around the world. But the experimental phase should now be giving way to production-level systems, ready to take on the information needs of the large numbers of people we serve. Experimentation should continue, and I think it always will, but that can't be all we do.

PLANNING TO PLAN MEANS HAVING A VISION

Before I get into the nuts and bolts of things to think about, I want to address two fundamental, overarching concerns. Unless both of these are addressed satisfactorily, I think any attempt at reenvisioning a reference service will likely fail.

First, Fit the Mission

First, whatever you plan and try should fit with the mission of your institution and your existing service. If this sounds somewhat trite and fatuous, that's because it's true. Regardless of whether you serve a geographic, academic, corporate, organizational, or intellectual community, you've got to make sure that whatever you do will work to achieve its objectives, especially as those objectives evolve in an increasingly wired and electronic world. In a corporate setting, being able to advance the bottom line is vital. Perhaps a service that leverages use of the corporate library or intranet would be of particular help. In an academic community, deans and faculty will value serving users participating in distance learning or students working from home at all hours of the day. Public libraries that extend beyond the reach of their walls and allow people to make use of their collections and resources regardless of constraints of time and distance will have more support from their communities, which may well translate into increased support in general.

This implies a fundamental level of political savvy. Services that are mounted because they're a good idea (à la the Judy Garland–Mickey Rooney "let's put on a show" model) might well be fun for the staff and a challenge to plan and implement. But if they don't make any sense or fit in with what else is going on, they have little likelihood of real success.

This emphatically does *not* mean that you should set your sights low—quite the contrary. Planning a suite of digital reference services can often be exactly the lever that's needed to reimagine the rest of the services a library offers to its community, and I'm going to argue that that is one of its main, if somewhat clandestine, benefits.

Second, Achieve Buy-In from Staff and Administrators

This leads to my second concern: working to achieve buy-in from staff and administration. In some cases, neither of these will be necessary; in others, both will. But often, the impetus for doing new things will come either from the top or from the grass roots, and so somebody will have to be convinced that this is a worthwhile idea, valuable, and so on. Let's be frank: more than a few reference librarians are not supportive of digital reference efforts;

some will even work to make sure they don't succeed. I think this last group is a small minority, but I wouldn't underestimate its importance, nor would I ignore the legitimate concerns of people who think reference is just fine the way it is. They're wrong, as statistics and anecdote seem to be telling us from every direction, but they have to be included in the process, their ideas and concerns have to be taken seriously, and they should be helped to come to terms with where their skills, expertise, and attitudes fit in.

I do know from research I've conducted that people who feel the most positively about digital reference services are those who are most actively involved in answering questions (Janes, 2002). In that survey, the more questions people had personally answered using digital reference in the previous two weeks, the better they felt about it in general. I can't say, though, whether one of these causes the other or just that the people who feel good about it are also the ones who do it. But the relationship is a strong one, and perhaps exposing people to what it is and can do might be one way to help them to understand its potential and personal value.

It's also the case that a lot of people now running reference departments went to library school about the time I did, in the early '80s or thereabouts. I know that we had little instruction in technology in my program, and as reference librarians, we were not prepared well for a world that was going to completely change out from underneath us. (Curiously, this was the time when the cataloging world was being turned upside down by OCLC, cooperative services, and the rise of copy cataloging. Reference librarianship has always been just a tiny bit smug about that; it's our turn now to watch technology sweep through what we do, I guess.)

There are lots of dynamic reference administrators who are deeply engaged in the process of retooling their services to meet the needs of a dynamic and technologically aware populace. The rest have to be helped along. They need to be convinced that the expenditure will be justified, that significant numbers of people will be able to take advantage of the service being offered, that they can sell it to the board or the CEO or whoever controls the

purse strings, and that this project isn't going to unduly compli-
cate their lives. Good, creative answers to those concerns will go
a long way toward helping them to see their way clear to being
supportive.

A TEN-STEP PROCESS FOR PLANNING A REFERENCE SERVICE

Well, there are a lot more than ten things to think about, but I've
tried to capture the important features of the planning process in
ten chunks. I've addressed several of these already in previous chapters, so I'll focus here on things we haven't touched on yet. This
is by no means a foolproof, tried-and-true planning guide; I do
hope, though, that it can be a good framework for people to use
in thinking about and implementing new services. It's also not intended to be strictly linear; I imagine people will find themselves
often going back and forth and making decisions in later stages
here that will have an impact on decisions previously made, forc-
ing those decisions to be rethought, and so on. OK, enough cave-
ats—here goes.

Step 1: Analyze the Community and Its Information Needs

*Describe and analyze the community or organization and its in-
formation needs*

I started this book with a discussion of users and communities
for a reason. Reference services don't exist because reference librarians exist and need something to do (nice as it is that they
keep us off the streets). They exist to serve the needs of our communities of users in the situations in which they find themselves.

When thinking about planning and implementing a service, it's
easy to ignore this step and launch right into the cool stuff, like
picking software and designing Web pages and fliers and writing
press releases and learning new resources. But there have been nu-
merous examples of failed services that didn't take account of what

their users wanted and needed. So let's avoid that trap and think hard about who people are, where they are, what they need, and how they'd like to get service.

This is the first example of a way in which planning for a digital reference service might positively affect a library's or organization's overall profile. Perhaps there hasn't been a comprehensive examination of the user population in quite some time; here's your opportunity to do it. Have the demographics changed? How wired are people? Has there been substantial change in what a college or business is doing? What's the political environment like? What unique features, subpopulations, aspects, exist that distinguish your setting from others? Finding out and knowing the answers to these kinds of questions might well have benefits beyond planning a revised reference service.

Step 2: Describe the Overall Nature of the Service

Describe the overall nature of the information service, including its institutional home and the justification or rationale for the service.

Once you have a basic idea of users and their likely information needs, begin to think about how you might be best able to serve them. Think broadly here: go beyond what you do now and what you're familiar with, and consider new ways of serving *your* people and *their* needs.

Here's a thought exercise for you. Assume you had no information or reference services at all. Nobody had ever thought of them, and the notion of providing direct, mediated services was arising just now. What would those services look like? Don't get bogged down in detail at this stage; that'll come shortly. Write a paragraph or page or so and describe the ideal services that would meet your population's needs. Draw some pictures of Web sites or physical locations. Put yourself in the shoes of the users. Ask some members of your community; maybe have some focus groups or convene some design panels to have users (and nonusers) of your current services think together about what kinds of things they'd like. Let cost, feasibility, and the rest of your concerns wait—this is the time to fantasize, to think big and creatively.

Reference services as we know them today arose as a largely agrarian nation was industrializing, as education was becoming more common, as more information resources were being produced, and as those tools were becoming more sophisticated and complicated. We face another set of societal transformations now, and the information world is changing as well, so it's worth starting over to think broadly, creatively, originally, and fearlessly about what can be, apart from and above what has been.

This is also your chance to articulate why these kinds of service are necessary. They're likely going to have to be sold to somebody somewhere, so it's wise to begin thinking about how to justify the expense and work involved sooner rather than later. Here's also where you can begin to appeal to institutional or community mission, administrative and staff concerns, political necessities, and so on.

Step 3: Predict the Volume of Traffic

Predict the expected volume of traffic from the new service.

This one could turn out to be quite difficult, but I think it's a necessary step before going too much further. It might be hard to predict how people might use a service, especially if it looks significantly different from what they're used to, has lots more aspects, appeals to a wider audience, and so on. I suggest making some ballpark estimates; gauge your situation, community, and population against what you hear about similar settings (here's a place where listserv memberships and conferences can be of great use), and come up with what seems a reasonable figure to use in planning. Actually, several figures probably make sense, to bracket a range of possible responses. Perhaps you intend to phase in services one at a time, have soft openings to make sure everything's working OK before publicizing them widely, bring in different segments of your community at different times. Or you might just go for it and see what happens.

Several years ago, a lot of people were concerned that putting up an e-mail address or a Web form meant they were going to be inundated with 500 questions a day from all over the world. (I don't know where that number came from, but I heard it from lots of independent sources. Fascinating.) Anyway, it didn't happen, largely because most of the services were hidden or unpublicized. Not getting overwhelmed had a curious effect. Some people were really disappointed with their not achieving huge traffic, and a miniature backlash emerged: since they didn't get huge traffic, perhaps there wasn't huge demand, so maybe this wasn't such a good idea to begin with.

If anything, I suggest you shoot high: plan for a number you think is on the high side of your estimates. It'll be easier to plan for and publicize a higher number than to try to cut back or scramble to add resources if you've underplanned.

Step 4: Describe the Service Points

Describe service points to be offered and the relative mix among them.

This is the real crux of the plan. In truth, reference services have evolved slightly over the years to reflect demographic and social trends, new ideas in interviews and service provision, and other factors, but this is the most profound and sometimes wrenching transformation we've had to undergo in three quarters of a century.

Information services can be provided to communities in different ways: reference desks where people visit in person, phone-based services, e-mail addresses or Web forms for sending in questions, chat or instant-messaging applications, call-center-based services, even video, voice-over IP, and no doubt more exotic things yet to come. Each has its own strengths and weaknesses, appeals to different users (and, for that matter, to different staff members), will be more or less appropriate in a given community for a given information need or situation.

And this is precisely the point; there's no *one* solution. For a very long time, we had two options: if patrons wanted to use an information service to get help, they could visit that service or call it on the phone. (Yes, there was always the option of sending mail, but that correspondence was a very small part of the vast majority of services.) Each of these was a synchronous interaction between the inquirer and the service's staff and typically resulted in some sort of immediate response, with the option of following up at a later time, perhaps using a different mode of interaction (faxing a response, mailing it, asking a phone inquirer to visit in person, calling back a patron who had come to a desk, and so on).

Users chose between these two options based on their inclination, the specific need in question, and the availability of the service (likely closed more than it was open and certainly not available after the evening or on much of the weekend), among other factors. They probably had a reasonably good suspicion of how each of these options would work and how the interaction would go, assumed they were likely to get an immediate or very quick response, and were likely to have a conversation of sorts with another person in the course of being assisted.

This all assumes they approached a service in the first place, of course. We know that using libraries or similar information services was never first on most people's lists of how to find information. They'd consult themselves, their own information, friends, contacts, and so on, before they'd approach the library. So the people who approached were desperate or feckless or both, pretty highly motivated to get a response, or habitual users of libraries who valued the kinds and levels of services they had to offer.

Now, of course, things have changed. There are many more ways in which we can make information services available to our users and communities. In fact, the array of potential avenues into our services can be a bit bewildering, even to a few librarians. We've been experimenting quite a bit with all of them, usually singly but occasionally in combination, trying to see what kinds of things seem to be working, popular, and so on.

The one thing that seems clearest to me at this point is that there's no one right way to do it. Not every user is going to want to use, say, chat technology, either in general or for any specific question. The same could be said for e-mail, Web forms, phone, face-to-face, or anything else. The same could also be said for librarians and for information needs, for that matter. It was always true, to be honest, but we only had a couple of options, so it was less obvious that one size didn't fit all.

So now that we have lots of sizes, so to speak, what do we do with them? Easy: use 'em all. Or at least all the ones that make sense. Once you know who your users are, where they are, what they want, what they're like, and what they're likely to want to use, the kinds of services you want to provide to satisfy their needs, and the likely volume of those needs, it is possible for you to look at the panoply of options and make some professional decisions. You might decide, for example, that your population is in a single physical location and there's lots of foot traffic, so a familiar walk-up reference desk is a major service point for you. You might look at your current gate statistics and decide you want to focus your energies and resources on a joint e-mail-and-chat service, perhaps reducing the staffing or hours of a desk or phone-based service. You could decide just about anything you want, so long as it's the right thing for your institution, community, users, and so on.

The central question here is not, "Should we get rid of the reference desk?" or "Should we try a call-center software package?" The central question is, "What is the optimal allocation of our effort and resources to provide the highest quality service for *our* users and *their* needs?" This has been the central question since the beginning, but we're just out of the habit of asking it, since the technological domain and environment haven't changed that radically in several generations.

So here's where you get to look across a wide span of service points (desk, phone, e-mail, Web, chat, and so on) and decide how much emphasis, staff, resources, training, and all the rest you will place with each. This will obviously involve a lot of guesswork and planning, and you'll almost certainly have to tweak it as you go and once you implement the service, but put a few stakes in the ground at this point, think big but realistically, and then proceed.

Step 5: Determine Staffing and Training Needs

Determine the service's staffing and training needs.

I addressed this already extensively in the previous chapter, so I won't belabor the point here.

Step 6: Determine Resource Needs

Determine other resources required: financial, space, informational, technological, and so on.

The most vital class of library resources is professional librarians, but those professionals have to be supported in several ways beyond the training I discussed previously. Supporting information services will likely be a nontrivial expenditure. Beyond budgeting for staff time, benefits, training, and so on, there will be other financial expenditures: for space and perhaps its renovation or conversion, hardware and software, information resources, publicity, evaluation, and so on. Beyond a mere budget, state the justification for each item, tied to the aims and goals of the service, the mission of the institution or community, and so on. Difficult questions are going to be asked, especially by whoever holds the purse strings, about why this expenditure will be necessary, how it will improve the service, how that improvement will be assessed, and what the benefit for the cost will be.

If, as is likely, more financial resources are necessary than are currently allocated, those questions will be sharper. It won't be enough to say that this new service will be hip and cool; more precise and focused answers will be necessary.

You should also plan for the time it will take to complete the development, deployment, training, publicity, maintenance, and evaluation. There will be financial implications for this time, of course, but the time itself should be budgeted in its own right, particularly if there are any volunteer or pro bono components to it.

New or revised information resources may also be necessary or a good idea. They might be as simple as new print copies of a few old standby resources or as complicated as negotiating new licensing agreements with database vendors or other publishers. You should be thinking about what kinds of resources you will emphasize in this service—digital, locally produced, licensed, freely available Web based, and so on—and perhaps which ones would be of particular importance or interest in which facets of the service. Will you do document delivery? How? Will you scan print documents, fax them, mail them?

How will you work with licensed content, if at all? This looms large in many people's thinking about digital services in particular. The more engaged the professional community is with the vendors and publishers, the more likely it is that the community will be able to reach agreements that satisfy both. At present, the use of consortia, networks, cooperatives, systems, and other conglomerations of libraries to gain bargaining and negotiating muscle seems to be of significant benefit. Vendors are worried, quite rightly, about giving away the store, and we're worried about not being able to use these resources when we know they're among the better ways to help many people. Working through these issues and finding the right middle ground will be a significant challenge, but finding that middle ground will be a win all the way around. Platitudes, I know, but this will take time and hard effort to work through—no easy answers here.

You may also decide to develop new resources, including links to Web sites of particular interest to your users or community, FAQs or FARQs (Frequently Asked Reference Questions), pathfinders to quality resources of all kinds on common topics, not to mention frequently asked policy or procedural questions for your institution.

There might be substantial technological investment required: hardware (dedicated computers for enhanced service, perhaps even a server for large institutions, scanners, Web cams, microphones, high-speed or high-quality printers), software (special-purpose applications such as 24/7 Reference, LSSI, Convey, and QuestionPoint; other software for the design or development of a Web presence), or both.

Again, the resources questions don't—or shouldn't—get answered in a vacuum. Don't just ask for $10,000; plan for a great service, find out what you'll need to do it, and then work to get the resources you need.

Step 7: Develop a Marketing Plan

Determine how the service will be publicized.

I've heard this story so many times I can't tell you, in various flavors and guises. Library (or somebody at library) decides to do digital reference. E-mail address or Web form goes up, but concern about being overwhelmed leads to decision to bury the link, give it some really confusing name, or both. Librarians breathlessly (and, perhaps, a little fearfully) wait for questions to come pouring in from all corners of the globe. Very little pouring occurs. Disappointment. Conclusion reached that digital reference isn't all it's cracked up to be. Grrr.

This scenario makes me mad for lots of reasons, but the primary one is the conclusion. There is lots of evidence that a well-publicized (and well-planned and well-maintained) service can be enormously popular and successful and help out lots of people. A good example is the suite of services from the Cleveland Public Library (www.cpl.org), which includes both e-mail and chat-based services and was publicized by a substantial advertising and marketing campaign. They got a lot of traffic, but they wanted that traffic and were prepared for it and so were able to handle it and be successful at it.

There are lots of ways in which services can be publicized, ranging from the simple to the elaborate. Some libraries will be able to buy or get free publicity on radio (probably the most cost effective), on television, and in newspapers; others may well find that posters in the school hallway, bus signs, bookmarks, or even word of mouth is their best tactic. Certainly, having links to a service on every page of the library's Web site (including interior pages as well as catalog and database pages) is a must.

And why not go further? If your public library is the "information source for the community," as we often say, then shouldn't a link to an information service be on the city's or county's Web site? on the chamber of commerce's site? Similarly, why not on the main page of your school, college, university, intranet? Not only will this increase the visibility of these services (and, we hope, traffic), but it will also make it easier for potential users to find that service and increase the visibility of everything you do within your organization or community. And I mean more here than just the perfunctory link to "the Library." Get an icon or a link that says "Ask a Librarian" or "Get Professional Answers" or whatever makes sense in your environment.

Yes, that probably means you'll get more traffic. The concern about being overwhelmed is a real and significant one, and I don't want to dismiss it out of hand. Most libraries and reference services are operating on pretty lean budgets, and a substantial increase in traffic and demand will strain those budgets and resources even further. But isn't the point of those budgets to serve the community? At the very least, a large increase in demand and traffic helps a library to make a case to whoever pays the bills that more resources are necessary to provide these vital services to the community and its clientele. The answer could well be no, and in difficult financial times it will often be no, but at least we have a stronger hand and can make a viable request and make the case that what we do is important and seen to be important by the people who use the service. And frankly, I'd rather be overwhelmed than bored any day, and I suspect most reference librarians feel the same way. It beats sitting at the desk reading through collection-development stuff or surfing the Web, waiting for people to stop by.

Step 8: Determine How the Service Will Be Evaluated

Determine how the new service will be evaluated and by whom.

In addition to planning to publicize the service, you must also plan to evaluate and assess how it is performing. Evaluating reference services is tricky business, and I don't intend here to get mired in the whole question of whether quality or satisfaction is the more significant criterion. Both are significant—can't we make people happy *and* be right all at the same time? But I digress.

There appears to be very little assessment and evaluation going on. In the survey I did of reference librarians last year, only 9 percent reported they had any systematic evaluation of their digital reference service (Janes, 2002). That's embarrassing and, moreover, does a disservice to us and to the people we serve.

So let's do better. There are a number of dimensions on which you could imagine evaluating your service; here are a few examples:

- Accuracy—still a good idea. Perhaps in follow-up—for training as well as evaluation—answers can be double-checked for accuracy, completeness, and so on.
- Number of questions received and answered—a simple but good measure of traffic and performance.
- Satisfaction—also important.
- Time to respond—average, median. This is also an opportunity to look at the kinds of questions that get answered really quickly and really slowly, to find out why and how to improve.
- Kinds of questions—by subject area, by type (homework, business development, local history, research, ready reference, and so on).
- Kinds of users—local/out of area, student/faculty/staff, area within organization.
- Repeat users—both individuals and the proportion of the overall number.
- New users—where they come from, how many per week/month/year.
- Dollars expended—overall, per question, per user.

I think that evaluation will be easier in many ways in the digital realm than in any other, because usually there is an artifact or trace. Transcripts of chat sessions and e-mail exchanges can be studied, statistics can be gathered from log files, and quick surveys can be sent following the response. In fact, we might even get higher-quality data from surveys we send two or three days or so afterward. It's very difficult to ask people to fill out surveys or questionnaires immediately following an in-person encounter;

it can be awkward because of the interpersonal nature of the exchange, and it's even more problematic over the phone. But a message that says something like "Hello. You asked us a question a couple of days ago, and now that you've had a chance to think about it, we'd like to know a little bit about how we did" and follows up with a few questions on accuracy, satisfaction, willingness to return, where the user heard about the service, and so on, might provide a more natural way to get at some of this data. There has been some evidence, from services like AskERIC and the IPL, that many responses come in from people who love the service and from those who hate it, without much of a middle ground. That might not always be the case, but it might be worth taking into account when evaluating data from these sorts of mechanisms.

One final point on evaluation: when you generate these kinds of data it's one thing to just look at the results and see how it's going, and there's nothing wrong with that, but I agree with Chuck McClure and Dave Lankes, who have been urging people to think beyond simple evaluation to performance standards. It's nice to be able to say that you answer 65 percent of your questions within 48 hours or that 72 percent of people would recommend your service to others, but without standards or targets to compare those figures to, they don't mean much.

Wouldn't it be better to say that your ambition is to have a service that responds to 75 percent of requests within 24 hours with an accuracy rate of 90 percent, generating 25 new users per week with 75 percent of users saying they'd recommend the service to a friend? There's nothing magical about those numbers (though you ought to shoot high, of course), but setting down standards like those *before* the service opens will give you something to aim at, and once those targets are reached, they can then be raised. Since part of the mission here is to provide a high-quality service, since that is a major distinguishing characteristic of library services, this kind of standards setting is crucial.

Step 9: Explore Relevant Policy Issues

Explore policy issues related to both the new service as well as its relationship to existing services.

There are a number of areas in which policy development can be important. Again, each service and institution is different, and each will make different decisions, to be sure, but there are a few areas that would be common to almost any service and domain.

What users will you serve? This is a legitimate question, and many people have been concerned about responding to questions from people who don't pay for the service. You might well decide not to, but of course this would eliminate participating in any sort of cross-institutional cooperative service. Librarians have always been pretty willing to cooperate and share—witness the widespread use of interlibrary-loan services—so I think that most libraries will be open to the idea of extending that notion to the reference domain. I also presume that the vast majority of libraries will answer a reference question posed in person or over the phone without asking for a library-card number or proof of membership in the service population. To be sure, it's much easier to pop off an e-mail to a library halfway across the country or around the world for that matter, so each library will have to decide for itself what to do here.

Many libraries do say that their services are reserved (either exclusively or primarily) for people who pay the freight: residents, members of the academic community, card holders, members of the corporation or organization. Many also say that they will respond to questions from anyone about their community, institution, collection, area, or unique resources. Some say that they'll respond to questions from outside these groups as time and resources permit.

The next logical question is how and whether to authenticate or verify membership in these communities. Some libraries do this by asking for or requiring library card numbers, PIN, or passwords. Others allow questions only from computers they recognize, using IP address verification or the use of a proxy server. Some ask for a local phone number, ZIP code, or address to verify residence. (It's true, of course, that remote users could manufacture a local phone number or ZIP code easily enough; I've always thought that such people have shown enough initiative to get themselves service regardless of where they are.)

The tradeoff here is between creating a service that will serve the needs of your community first, as you should rightly do, and creating barriers to that service, even to people who are paying for it. Residents without library cards, students off campus, members of the corporation not on the intranet—all still "deserve" the service but may not be able to verify themselves adequately, so provisions might need to be made for those kinds of contingencies.

What kinds of questions will you answer? The major division here is between answering brief, factual, ready-reference-type questions and answering deeper, more research-oriented questions. A number of libraries and librarians, concerned about the interview or lack thereof, have emphasized answering the quicker questions on the theory that they require less of an interview and are therefore more suitable. I've already disagreed with that in several places, so I'll just say again here that I don't believe that's true. The question about what kinds of inquiries to respond to should have much more to do with mission, users, communities, and needs than technology.

That said, there are some kinds or areas of questions that are often handled differently or separately. Most libraries shy away from answering questions of a legal or medical nature or on tax matters, preferring instead to provide general sources and suggest people consult a professional. I would note, as an aside, though, that particularly in the case of medical inquiries, a lot of people are turning to the Web as a major source of health information and may therefore be particularly looking for help or guidance in this area. I'm not at all suggesting libraries answer these kinds of questions, as we are almost always unqualified to do so, but I do think we might get a larger number of these questions via the Web than in person, and libraries should be prepared for it and have good policies in place for how to respond to or refer those inquiries. Genealogy questions are also often seen as "different," and these inquiries are often referred to the local or state historical society, genealogical Web sites, or services such as ancestry.org, and so on.

In some cases, I've seen libraries describe or discuss their services in terms unfamiliar to most laypeople. Telling people that the service will accept "any question you might ask at the reference desk of any public library" or "questions we can answer without further input from you" or that the library will spend up to 20 minutes answering a question doesn't really help someone who isn't a professional librarian or doesn't know intimately how such a service works. You should describe your service and policies in clear language easily understandable by your clientele.

How long will you take to answer? From what I've seen, there's a lot of fuzziness about this: "Our goal is to respond to all inquiries with 48 hours." "We strive to answer all questions within a day or two." I know that people writing such statements think they're being helpful and are trying not to raise expectations that can't be met, which I can sympathize with, but it can also come across as more than a little feckless. Especially this one, which is a close paraphrase of one I actually read: "Our service goal is to respond to all questions within three to five business days, unless the question comes in on a Friday or weekend, in which case we'll treat it as though it came in on the following Monday." That sounds just awful and translates, to me at least, as "Go away. We're pretty slow." I also think this service said it would only answer ready-reference questions. Sigh.

I've seen turnaround-time policies ranging from 24 hours or so to several days; my favorite said, "You will get an answer from us within 24 hours, probably less." Love it. That inspires confidence and makes somebody want to use the service. Several libraries I've seen also include phone numbers for quicker service.

I'd say you should be realistic in what you say but not wishy-washy, take into account what the service is for, the people being served, the kinds of questions they're likely to ask, the environment, the resources at hand, and all the rest we've talked about, and let the policies flow from that framework. And if it sounds bad, make it better by finding more or new resources, tweaking the service, rethinking the plan, or whatever makes sense.

In addition, you should strongly consider developing policies on

- confidentiality and the privacy of questions and answers—people have a right to know what, if anything, will happen to these, whether their names, e-mail addresses, phone numbers, and other personal information will be stored, who will have access to it, what might be done with it, if any kind of research will or could be performed using this data, and so on;
- fees for items mailed, faxed, or otherwise delivered, plus fees for the use of materials from licensed databases for out-of-service-population users, paying attention to the provisions of licensing agreements;
- types of resources you will or won't use in responding to inquiries;
- hours and days of the service, if applicable; and
- who will answer questions (professionals, paraprofessionals/technical staff, subject experts, staff at other institutions)—

and tell potential users about them.

If you know the kinds of information needs your users are likely to have and the resources available to you to use in responding to them, then policies like these should naturally fall into place. There will likely be iteration in your planning—as you get down to the policy stage, for example, you may discover that you need new training or staffing or that more or different resources will be required. Your timetable (see below) may be too ambitious. Your quality standards may be too low. That's OK; in fact, it's probably a good thing, as it means that your overall plan is improving and coming closer to fruition. And it's probably never really done, as the results of your evaluation are fed back into the service for improvement and refinement.

Step 10: Develop an Implementation Schedule

Lay out an implementation schedule with major milestones.

Nothing really special or magical here—just a good idea for

planning purposes. If you're the type who goes in for that sort of thing, you can use software like Microsoft Project to make schedules, including staff, other resources, and so on. This sort of schedule often helps to keep things on track and give you a sense of how it's going, especially when it includes a target date for completion of the project or individual phases.

PLAN FOR SUCCESS

If I could leave you with only one thing after reading this chapter, it'd be this: plan for success. Avoid incrementalism. Develop a service that meets the information needs of your users and community, and integrate all the pieces so they work together in a seamless way. Then give it the resources it needs, publicize it widely and wisely, and be ready for people to come and use it. Assume that it will be successful in terms of both performance and traffic. Plan for a pattern of growth, including adding resources as necessary.

I'm not talking here about small change; I'm talking about a significant and meaningful revision of the way we think about providing information services to our clientele, perhaps the first one in generations. And we can't really afford for this to be a timid affair. We all know, deep down inside, that our users are drifting even further away from the use of library services. With every passing day, more people are thinking of the Internet as a trusted and easy-to-use source of information for many of their needs. There's nothing wrong with that; in fact, it's a tremendous opportunity not only for them but for libraries and librarians as well.

Librarians and libraries, though, stand for something more. We stand for quality, for service, for selection, and for all the other values we've discussed. We need our services to succeed so that we can help those values to persist. It's not important that libraries as organizations survive, though I hope they do. It is important that what libraries stand for and achieve survives, so that our society and civilization persist and thrive. One significant way in which we can ensure that is to be a vital and vibrant part of the information lives of the members of our communities; the more they think of us as a trusted and easy-to-use information source, the more we succeed.

So let's do it.

QUESTIONS FOR REVIEW

- What lessons can the reference world learn from the cataloging and technical-services experiences of the last 20 years?
- What techniques could be used to estimate the volume of traffic in a new digital reference service?
- Why do we seem to have such problems with marketing our services?
- Why do we seem to have such problems with evaluating our services?
- What does success look like, in this context?

REFERENCES

Biblarz, Dora, Stephen Bosch, and Chris Sugnet. 2001. "Scenarios for User Needs Assessments." In *Guide to Library User Needs Assessment for Integrated Information Resource Management and Collection Development*, edited by Dora Biblarz, Stephen Bosch, and Chris Sugnet. Lanham, Md.: Scarecrow Press, 43–50.

Blattberg, Robert C., Gary Getz, and Jacquelyn S. Thomas. 2001. "The Marketing Mix." In *Customer Equity: Building and Managing Relationships as Valuable Assets*, edited by Robert C. Blattberg, Gary Getz, and Jacquelyn S. Thomas. Boston: Harvard Business School Press, 147–60.

Church, Doug. 1998. "Filling the Planning Vacuum." *Information Outlook* 2, no. 2 (February) 34–36.

Fagan, Jody Condit, and Michele Calloway. 2001. "Creating an Instant Messaging Reference System." *Information Technology and Libraries* 20, no. 4 (December).

Greenberg, Paul. 2001. "Customer Lifetime Value." In *CRM at the Speed of Light*. New York: McGraw-Hill, 343–49.

Greenberg, Paul. 2001. "Implementing CRM: Easy as 1,2,3,4,5,6, and So On." In *CRM at the Speed of Light*, 281–301.

Hegenbart, Barbara. 1998. "The Economics of the Internet Public Library." *Library Hi-Tech* 16, no. 2: 69–83.

Horn, Judy. 2001. "The Future Is Now: Reference Service for the Electronic Era." In *Crossing the Divide: ACRL Tenth National Conference, Denver Colorado, March 15–18*, 320–27.

Janes, Joseph. 2002. "Digital Reference: Reference Librarians' Experiences and Attitudes." *Journal of the American Society for Information Science and Technology* 53, no. 7 (May): 549–66.

Janes, Joseph, and Chrystie Hill. 2002. "Finger on the Pulse: Librarians Describe Evolving Reference Practice in an Increasingly Digital World." *Reference & User Services Quarterly* 42, no. 1 (autumn): 54–65.

Lipow, Anne, and Steve Coffman. 2001. "Developing Your Service Policies." In *Establishing a Virtual Reference Service: VRD Training Manual*. Edison, N.J.: LSSI, 1–10, module 2.

Weissman, Sara. 2001. "Considering a Launch?" *Library Journal* 126, no. 2 (February): 49.

Weissman, Sara. 2001. "Know Your Audience." *Library Journal Net Connect* (spring): 42.

White, Marilyn Domas. 2001. "Digital Reference Services: Framework for Analysis and Evaluation." *Library and Information Science Research* 23, no. 3 (January): 211–31.

Chapter 7

Syncope

In this final chapter, I don't want to summarize so much as encapsulate and reiterate some of what I've been trying to say throughout the book.[1] (Translation: you can't just read this to get the whole picture, but you will find many of these themes repeated throughout.) I'll finish up with a brief vision of one way in which we might reconceive how we offer services.

So, in no particular order—

PLAY TO OUR PROFESSIONAL STRENGTHS

Whatever we do should *play to our strengths as a profession*. This includes the values we subscribe to: intellectual freedom, a commitment to educating people as well as simply answering questions. It also means that we should be concerned about evaluation and quality of information sources; use sophisticated tools and techniques for searching; understand the nature of our users, their communities, their needs and situations; compile and organize and package information resources for their use; help them to understand how to help themselves and how to use and evaluate information. These, the goals and motivations of reference librarians for over a century, would lead us to a school of reference librarianship less focused on the answers to specific questions and more on providing assistance and support to people with more detailed, more demanding, more comprehensive information needs of all kinds, from the personal to the professional, from the mundane to the cosmic.

I wonder if perhaps the introduction of easy-to-use ways of finding things on the Internet might spell the most profound change for information services in libraries. If people are able to use Google and Yahoo! and other tools to find answers to basic ready-reference questions, then it follows that fewer of those questions will present themselves to library reference services. Moreover, using those tools is likely to be quicker than even the best, most responsive reference service. To be sure, people use search engines badly, get way too many results or way too few or things that are completely off the mark or wrong. These phenomena seem not to have diminished their traffic or popularity, though. I've certainly worked with people on reference desks and in digital reference environments who have tried search engines and failed, but that is precisely where librarians should come in: helping people who are unable to help themselves to use these and, for that matter, any other information tools.

Although it gives me no pleasure to say it, I think we may be the last generation of reference librarians to concentrate on ready reference as a major component of their work lives. I think what we call "ready reference"—quick, factual answers to specific questions—will always be a part of librarianship, but a diminishing part, and in the information world that looks to be emerging, it doesn't make a lot of sense to have that as a primary focus.

A recent study from the Pew Internet and American Life Project indicates that millions of Americans are using the Internet for major life decisions, such as getting more education, changing careers, making a major purchase, helping a loved one through a serious illness, or making a major investment.[2] Academic librarians know that students as well as faculty are turning online for research in their work. And that turn isn't just to the free Internet; it also includes licensed databases with access to full text, electronic books, and other expensive digital resources. All of these combine to put much greater power in the hands of users, a power many of them are unable or unwilling to exercise completely, leading to an even greater need for professional assistance when the stakes are high or the pressure is on or they simply get overwhelmed or lost.

This all reinforces the notion that reference librarianship ought to *stop chasing ready reference* and move toward a more efficient application of our unique skills, talents, perspectives, training, and experience. Perhaps we should declare victory and move on. People are getting answers to and help with many of their simple information needs without our intervention. Let's call that a good thing—and even if those answers and that help are what we would consider substandard or less than it could be, there doesn't appear to be a whole lot we can do about it—and promote the heck out of the great services we offer, present and future, that can't be gotten anywhere else.

We should also *make it really easy to use our services*. And I mean really easy. Because we have always known that most people won't try very hard to get a good answer, and if they don't have to try very hard at all to get a good-enough answer, that'll be— well—good enough. Since we're aiming to be more than good enough, we have to be that much easier to use and to find. Put links to your service everywhere. Promote it like crazy.

This all presumes you know who your users are and what they want. I've harped on them a lot, so here are two more important aspects to consider. First of all, if you truly know who they are, you also know where they are, geographically as well as psychically. And we need to *be where they are*. That means we need to be handy and easy to get to when they have an information need (hence linked in many, many places), but we also need to be in their minds and thoughts when they have that need. The more we can get people to think of libraries in all their various incarnations and instantiations when they have a question or a problem, the more we are likely to be able to be of help and thus provide that help.

Increasingly, this also means we need to *use the tools they're using*. If your user community is highly wired, you probably want to think hard about a chat-based service, e-mail, increased use of the Web, and so on. If the corporate intranet is the way in which things get done and information gets conveyed, use it, and be there.

Wireless, PDAs, PCS devices common on your campus? Use them. Don't we want, for example, a student meandering from her classrooms to her dorm room, pondering something that came up in class or looking for a good place to have coffee or dinner, surfing the Web on her cell phone, to think of asking her college or public library, connect directly to it in some way, and get an answer? That'd be pretty cool, and she'll think the world of that service. In fact—no, to be honest, she probably won't; she won't give it a second thought, and that's probably even better. Being a seamless part of her information world would be a huge achievement, and I hope we get there some day.

This is a great opportunity for reference librarians to *innovate and lead*—perhaps one of the best opportunities we've had in a very long time. There are so many possibilities of things we can do, ways in which we can think in new ways about services we could provide, modes of serving people, technologies we could try, communities we could reach in ways we never could before. It staggers the imagination to think what could happen if we seized these chances.

With these opportunities come responsibilities and obligations. We have to *plan for the success of our services* by identifying and securing the resources we need to make them work for the level of traffic that will make a difference in the information lives of users in the communities we serve. There's no sense, at this stage, in putting together some measly add-on service that hasn't remotely got the staff or money or other resources it needs to work. We need to be very public and very loud about these new services and *not hide them or weasel around* about what kinds of questions we'll answer or how long we'll take to answer them. We have always had great services to offer, and we've all had the nearly daily experience of people saying, "Wow! I had no idea a library could help me with this!" Whose fault is that, precisely? Let's not let that happen anymore.

We also have the obligation to *evaluate our services* in a meaningful way, and not just to see how we're doing but also to help us to move forward toward specific targets and levels of service, satisfaction, performance, accuracy, and so on. A crucial part of that kind of evaluation is also evaluation of the performance of individuals in these services. We have to incorporate notions of peer review, self-evaluation based on the evidence we get from transcripts and other artifacts produced by electronically mediated services. It's not going to do any good to embarrass people, publicly or privately, by picking over their transcripts, but it's amazing what you can see when you look at some of these.

Other professions do this as a matter of course, and reference librarians have been able to skate by without meaningful consistent evaluation for a very long time because the work we do has been ephemeral and difficult to pin down. Now we're freed from that problem, and we can make ourselves better as a profession as a result. There are some librarians who are concerned about this kind of evaluation and shy away from using digital reference techniques for this, among other, reasons. Some of them are probably just fine but concerned about having other people looking over their shoulder, and I can understand that. But there are others who are concerned for likely very good reasons, and if peer review, self-reflection, training, and other techniques to help people be good reference librarians fail, these people should probably find other work to do, to make themselves and their patrons happier.

One final opportunity is the chance to *work with other librarians in cooperative services*. This has the potential to completely make over reference librarianship. We've all struggled with inquiries that we know *somebody* would know how to deal with more effectively, and we've overheard colleagues describing questions they worked on unsuccessfully and we've known the answer and where to find it immediately. That's really frustrating. Moreover, if we were able to capture the collective knowledge and experience of an entire library staff or that of a network, state, region, or beyond, the level and quality of service we could provide as a result would be staggering. The early evidence from collaborative services is good, but there's much more work to be done, standards and protocols to be developed, and practice to be evolved. The prize is so attractive, though, that this hard work will be worth it.

Much good work has been done over the past several years in

this area, and I commend all the reference librarians who have toiled, often with little or no resources other than their own time, a good idea, and the support of their colleagues, to try new things and learn what works and what doesn't. I have always been impressed with the tenacity and innovation of the library community, and this recent work is yet a further example of our best characteristics. Sadly, however, it's not always as easy as that. A number of people, especially people who entered the profession some time ago, are less than pleased with some aspects of the new turns that reference librarianship is taking. I can understand and even sympathize with this. A lot of people became reference librarians because they were good at it, liked the thrill of the chase, liked knowing the sources and helping people find answers and the give-and-take of the interaction.

And then it all changed, seemingly overnight, and there didn't seem to be a whole lot we could do about it. It's a scary prospect when your profession drops out from underneath you, and many of our colleagues weren't prepared well, either by their professional education or by their personal inclinations, to deal with this kind of rapid and profound change. No wonder they're displeased and even fearful. Heck, even I'm scared sometimes. This concern takes many forms, but the one I've heard the most often is about the lack of a reference interview in digital environments. It is absolutely true that using e-mail or chat or other kinds of technologies means that the reference interview we all were familiar and comfortable with[3] won't be possible anymore. That does not mean, however, that there aren't or can't be effective ways of determining someone's information needs using digital technologies.

We need to *get over the reference interview and other perceived impediments* to trying new things in reference. Sure, we don't know how to do a high-quality reference interview in the chat environment yet. That's because we haven't been trying for very long. We didn't figure out how to do good reference interviews in person or via telephone immediately, either. It's going to take time to try these things out, to see what works and what doesn't and what kinds of techniques seem to be useful. We need to fail a lot and learn from those mistakes. Most important, we need to share these findings with one another, through research and presentations, so that we can learn together and improve our services.

BEGIN BY STARTING OVER

My final word? *Start over.* (OK, two words.) Here's my modest proposal, which I offer as a way of thinking about what you could do next.

Assume you'd never offered any kind of "reference" service before. Assume you'd never even heard of it, that the idea never crossed your mind. You've been amassing collections for your communities, organizing them well, making them available, but the whole place has been a big self-service buffet. No reference desk. No courses in library school. Nothing.

Now, today, in the early twenty-first century, it dawns on us all, as it did on our predecessors in the nineteenth, that it might be a good idea to help people out when they're confused. It was easy to conceive and develop service models in the nineteenth century because there were only two ways to interact with people: they came in, or perhaps they wrote the occasional letter. Everything else—the desk, the specialized resources, the telephone, all the accoutrements that we think of as natural and inevitable—slowly accreted over the decades. So a lot of what we think of when we think of reference work is based on that original work that's just been passed down from generation to generation, with embellishments and improvements, for a century and a quarter.

I think it's time to take a fresh stab at this. Look around at your community. Who are its members? Where are they? What do they want? How can they get at you? How can you make yourself available to them easily, quickly, and in a professional way?

You'll probably come up with several answers. You'll likely decide that the reference desk still makes sense, but perhaps staffed differently than you're used to. I imagine many libraries will envision a variety of approaches using technology from the telephone to videoconferencing. Those are all good, and each library and staff will make decisions among these and the relative mix of staffing and resources.

Now, once you've made those decisions, you need to present these options to your clientele in such a way that individual users can make sense of them and make intelligent decisions about them. Here's an example, which I completely made up, of text you might have on a Web page or flier:

You can ask us questions in several ways:

If you need a quick answer,
- you can call us at 363–3050 between 9:00 a.m. and 7:00 p.m. each day. You'll speak to a staff member who can work with you for a few minutes to find an answer. If we don't find it, then we'll suggest you send us e-mail or stop in for further help.
- you can use the Internet to *chat with a staff member* between 4:00 p.m. and 11:00 p.m. weekdays.

If you have a more detailed question, and need an answer quickly,
- we recommend visiting the library to work in person with a reference librarian. Our library hours are 9:00 a.m. to 7:00 p.m. each day. We'll be able to spend more time with you than on the phone or chat and will work with you to provide the best answer we can while you're in the library.

If you have a more detailed question and have a little more time,
- you can send us a question *via a Web form*. This form will ask you a number of things to help us help you with your request. We'll be able to do more and deeper searching and will get a response to you within 24 hours. We might send you e-mail or call you to clarify what you need. If your question is particularly challenging, we may ask if you wish it be forwarded to a service staffed by librarians around the world for further help; this might take another 2 or 3 days.

This certainly isn't perfect and certainly wouldn't be exactly the right thing for any specific library, but I think it has some things going for it. It tells people what their options are based on their situation and need and what's likely to happen based on the choice that *they* make about how to pose their question. It doesn't describe services so much as situations, free of library jargon no layperson understands, and allows people to make up their own minds about how to approach the library's services, which appear relatively seamless to them. It also lets them know that their request might get moved around, from one aspect of the service to another, based on the librarian's best professional estimate of how to handle it. We give them multiple entry points to the service, but then we can take charge and switch to a more appropriate way of responding, if necessary.

Some inquirers will choose an entry point based on personal inclination or preference: some people may always want to chat or call or visit. Sometimes, they'll make a choice based on time or other constraints—if they need an answer immediately, they might chat. Sometimes, it'll be based on their situation or connectivity—they're on a cell phone and can only call.

The same will be true on the library's end. Some librarians will prefer certain ways of working and focus on e-mail or the desk. Some requests will be more or less appropriate for a given mode because of time, connectivity, and so on. Some librarians will have or develop certain areas of subject expertise and thus focus on requests across modes in those areas; this would particularly develop, I would guess, in cooperative services. We will also find ourselves increasingly using new resources or familiar ones in new ways, including organizations (via e-mail, listservs), experts and other individuals (via e-mail, listservs, ask-an-expert services), pathfinders, lists of frequently asked questions, and so on.

That's it. Nothing earth-shaking, I know, but it might spark a few ideas of your own and help you to think about what you might do to best serve your community.

FINAL THOUGHTS: "ALL THESE THINGS AND MORE"

I was born to be a reference librarian. I know this because I set up a library in my room at home when I was growing up; I felt at home the first time I ever stood behind a reference desk; I never use the index to *The World Almanac:* I can find things more quickly based on where I know they are because my mother bought me one for Christmas every year, and I spent the next week reading it. She was a reference librarian, too, one of the best I ever knew, and even without a master's degree, she taught me a lot about how to be a good one.

I tell my students and potential applicants to our program that there's no better job in the world than to be a reference librarian. We make humanity more human. We help our users and communities find what they need to help them, satisfy their curiosity, be better people. It's easy to get trapped in the mundane part of what we do and think that we're just helping undergraduates find articles for papers, high school kids do their homework, people fix their cars, and so on, but it's really more than that. Librarians in general help humanity to tell its story to itself, and reference librarians are the grease in that wheel, pushing it along and making it easier on everyone involved. It's a magnificent thing to do, and I'm proud to be a part of it.

This profession that I cherish is very different now from what it was when I took my reference class in 1980 and will be very different still when my current students reach their twentieth anniversaries in the profession. Or at least I hope it will be. When the story is told, years from now, of how the Internet became part of librarianship and vice versa, I want it to be a story of professionalism, innovation, and success. I want to be able to say that we took on the challenge of figuring out what to do, did it, and did it well. The alternatives—doing nothing or doing small things in a timid or constrained way—are too terrible to contemplate, because I think we all know what the results will be if we take that path.

We will know we've succeeded when we stop using the phrase *digital reference.* For now, it's a convenient label for these kinds of efforts, and I use it as much as the next person. What's really going on, though, is just what reference librarians have been doing since the beginning, developing services that make good sense for their communities in the environment of the day.

By the way, we can keep calling what we do "reference," at least among ourselves. I don't think, however, that this is the right way to present our services to the wider world. It's a meaningless word to anybody other than librarians and a few dedicated library users and fans. True, people are used to seeing it, but that doesn't mean it's right or best. I don't have a suggestion for a new word or phrase, so I leave that up to you. I do think we need to have an easy way to identify what our services do and what they are to make them easier for people to understand, find, and use.

A lot is riding on this. I'm not exaggerating when I say that the future of libraries in general hangs on what we do in the next few years. We could become a vital and energetic part of the information lives of our communities. We could be the first thing community members think of when they have a question or an information need. Our services could be vibrant, making the best use of new technologies and the collective wisdom and expertise of skilled librarians around the world, providing high-quality services, educating people about information and its evaluation and use and how to help themselves more effectively. We could do all these things and more, and we should. We must. When we do, that is when will we truly succeed.

And, for the record, I believe we will.

QUESTION FOR REVIEW

- Do you?

ENDNOTES

1. syncope: "NOUN: **1.** *Grammar* The shortening of a word by omission of a sound, letter, or syllable from the middle of the

word; for example, *bos'n* for *boatswain.* **2.** *Pathology* A brief loss of consciousness caused by a temporary deficiency of oxygen in the brain; a swoon. See synonyms at <u>blackout</u>. ETYMOL-OGY: Middle English *sincopis*, from *sincopene*, from Late Latin *syncopn*, accusative of *syncop*, from Greek *sunkop*, from *sunkoptein*, to cut short : *sun–*, syn– + *koptein*, to strike." From *American Heritage Dictionary*, 4th ed. (2000). Available on the Web, of course, at: www.bartleby.com/61/58/S0965800. Both senses of the word seem appropriate as I write this final section . . .

2.   Pew Internet and American Life Project, "Use of the Internet at Major Life Moments," May 8, 2002. Available at: www.pewinternet.org/reports/toc.asp?Report=58.

3.   Well, many of us were comfortable with it, as we've seen—but there's considerable evidence it wasn't being done particularly often or well (Ross and Nilsen, 2000, for example).

REFERENCES

Ross, Catherine Sheldrick, and Kirsti Nilsen. 2000. "Has the Internet Changed Anything in Reference? The Library Visit Study, Phase 2." *Reference and User Services Quarterly* 40, no. 2 (winter): 147–55.

Index

About the Author

Joseph Janes is Associate Professor and Chair of Library and Information Science at the Information School of the University of Washington and Founding Director of the Internet Public Library. A frequent speaker in the U.S. and abroad, he is the co-author of eight books on librarianship, technology, and their relationship, and writes the "Internet Librarian" column for *American Libraries* magazine. Other Neal-Schuman titles that Dr. Janes has contributed to are *The Internet Searcher's Handbook: Locating Information, People, and Software* and *The Internet Public Library Handbook* (both 1999). Joseph Janes holds the M.L.S. and Ph.D. from Syracuse University, and has taught at the University of Michigan, the University of North Carolina at Chapel Hill, the State University of New York at Albany, as well as at Syracuse and Washington.